# STARTING FROM SCRATCH

# STARTING FROM
# SCRATCH

### ONE WOMAN'S PURSUIT OF
### FAMILY, BUSINESS, AND THE AMERICAN DREAM

## SHELLY L. HENDERSON
#### WITH PHIL HENDERSON

*Advantage*®

Published by Advantage, Charleston, South Carolina.
Member of Advantage Media Group.

ADVANTAGE is a registered trademark, and the Advantage colophon is a trademark of Advantage Media Group, Inc.

Printed in the United States of America.

10  9  8  7  6  5  4  3  2  1

ISBN: 978-1-59932-885-0
LCCN: 2018937730

Cover design by Melanie Cloth.
Layout design by Megan Elger.

This publication is designed to provide accurate and authoritative information in regard to the subject matter covered. It is sold with the understanding that the publisher is not engaged in rendering legal, accounting, or other professional services. If legal advice or other expert assistance is required, the services of a competent professional person should be sought.

Advantage Media Group is proud to be a part of the Tree Neutral® program. Tree Neutral offsets the number of trees consumed in the production and printing of this book by taking proactive steps such as planting trees in direct proportion to the number of trees used to print books. To learn more about Tree Neutral, please visit **www.treeneutral.com**.

Advantage Media Group is a publisher of business, self-improvement, and professional development books and online learning. We help entrepreneurs, business leaders, and professionals share their Stories, Passion, and Knowledge to help others Learn & Grow. Do you have a manuscript or book idea that you would like us to consider for publishing? Please visit **advantagefamily.com** or call **1.866.775.1696**.

*To Blake and Grant,*
*my love for you is like the opportunities in life: endless.*

# TABLE OF CONTENTS

-----------------------------------------------------

# ACKNOWLEDGMENTS

**TO MY APPALACHIAN STATE WOMEN'S GOLF TEAMMATES:** There is something special about belonging to a team, a common interest that binds us together. Your support and friendship has withstood the test of time and I am grateful for each of you, your leadership, and for our mutual love of the game. I am proud of the ones who continue to use what they learned as teammate and player in their career path to this day.

**TO APPALACHIAN STATE UNIVERSITY ATHLETICS:** Thank you for providing me with the experience to play collegiate golf. I am, to this day, beyond grateful for the opportunity I had to represent and play for the university. Being an athlete is so much more than what one sees on the field. It takes a unique individual with the will and dedication to excel both on the field and in the classroom.

**TO SIGMA KAPPA AND MY SORORITY SISTERS:** Fate took a good turn when I turned to you, the new chapter on campus with no reputation. I needed to try something new and you accepted me. I have lifelong friendships because of my sisterhood. You taught me about giving back and making a difference. To this day I "live with heart" in all that I do.

**TO MY LIFE GROUP:** Thank you for taking the chance and believing in me as your leader. Our time together every other week for almost three years has been rewarding. It is because of our efforts to grow our faith and ourselves that I was able to gain the confidence to write this book.

**TO FOREST HILL CHURCH:** In particular, David Chadwick and Rebecca Woodman. Sundays are better because of you, David Chadwick. You remind us that church is a community to enjoy with others and that we grow more in faith when we are together rather than alone. Rebecca Woodman, my new friend in Christ, so glad I had the courage to come talk to you! Our lives can change and have new meaning when we have the courage to open our minds and hearts to a different way of thinking. Thank you for helping me understand what life looks like when our minds and hearts have no limits and are open to the power of Jesus.

**TO SUMMER FLYNN:** Project Editor and my "Editor in Chief!" Thank you for teaming up with me to help me achieve my goal of writing a book. You inspired me and I miss our weekly phone calls! I look forward to our next project.

**TO MY MOTHER:** You continue to be a role model for all and I appreciate your work ethic and the desire to try new things the older you become. You are proof that it is never too late to learn or grow. Just like your mother always used to say, "age is just a number." You don't let that stop you! You are your best you at this season in your life.

**TO MY HUSBAND:** Who would have thought I would get to call you husband? We are better people because we have each other. My life is full because you continue to challenge and encourage me. Thank you for never letting our glass be half empty and for reminding me and the boys that where there is a will there is a way.

**TO PAST AND PRESENT HENDERSON PROPERTIES EMPLOYEES:** First, we are beyond grateful to the ones who have withstood the test of time. Every one of you have made us who we are today, both personally and professionally. To the ones who didn't stay very long, despite the circumstances, timing is everything. And to the newbies we presently have on staff, your timing is awesome!

**TO BABY WARREN ANDERSON HUNT**: Your sweet, short life was one of pure love and joy. Most spend their lives searching for a life of such perfection, yet never find it. To your parents, Logan and William Hunt, I honor you for your testament of what is truly important in this life. May you be abundantly blessed for the rest of your lives and let this be a reminder to us all:

> *"But it is not the length of life that counts—*
> *it is the depth and strength of life."*
>
> —Warren Wiersbe

# FOREWORDS

------------------------

**SHELLY HENDERSON IS MY DEAR FRIEND.** While we are both working moms, we first met through our children in 2012 and have shared much laughter over the years. The Shelly Henderson you meet in *Starting from Scratch* is the genuine expression and portrayal of the woman I am fortunate to know. I have seen, first hand, the many facets of Shelly. She is simultaneously a successful entrepreneur who can rock a business presentation or close a new business deal, the committed Mom who is a terrifyingly great football team parent, and the woman who has instilled deep and wonderful traditions in her family. Her boys, all three of them, adore her.

But don't get me wrong, this driven, hard-working, creative woman is not all work and no play! She can throw a mean football tailgate, hang on a beach, and camp (well, "glamp" anyway). Her 50th birthday party was a celebration of family and friends and the fun that all of us hope to have.

When she talks about building Henderson Properties, she often describes herself as having started from nothing. That's true when it comes to money, but far from true for Shelly's personal attributes. Shelly is smart, focused, energetic, and determined. She is full of love, and cares deeply for people. These are the raw materials that have made her successful as both an entrepreneur and as a Mom. Her story is one of courage, passion, and grit. I admire the honest look she provides here about her hard-earned success at work and within her family and how it comes down to characteristics we all have or can develop: the willingness to take risks, the discipline of unrelenting hard work, and a constant focus on making the world a better place.

And let's not forget that she built her company and her family at a time when there were few role models, and certainly no playbooks for work/life balance or how to achieve both professional and family success. What she has accomplished through forging her own path is genuinely important and impactful. Shelly is a true pioneer.

*Starting from Scratch* is well worth your time. Shelly Henderson's story will inspire you, encourage you, and validate that it is possible to be a whole person.

**Catherine P. Bessant**
Chief Operations and Technology Officer, Bank of America

--------------------------------------------------------------

**SHELLY'S JOURNEY OF ENTREPRENEURSHIP** might have started over two decades ago, but being her sorority sister, golf teammate, and roommate, I knew it was predestined. I have been fortunate to have Shelly as a friend from the minute I stepped on campus my freshman year at Appalachian State; our friendship has thrived for over 30 years. Being friends for so long is special and impactful. I knew Shelly's natural leadership skills and humility would lead her to success, and I have been watching it happen from a front row seat.

Knowing Shelly for over thirty years means I've known Phil for just as long. Within those years they were together for most of them, either dating, engaged, or married. I remember tagging along with them one spring afternoon as they drove around Boone and Blowing Rock looking at real estate when they were still in their early 20s and not even out of college yet. Somehow I knew, riding around with them that Saturday afternoon, they were going to be together and that both of them had the courage to chase a lion-sized dream.

Six years later, I was celebrating New Year's Eve with them in the newly renovated fixer upper, in the Plaza Midwood section of Charlotte. Ten years later I was visiting from Connecticut and I was riding around with them as they were looking at real estate in Boone and Blowing Rock again. This time they were looking to purchase that second home they had dreamed about back in their college days. About 22 years later, after a night of bowling and fun, they took me by a building that had a Henderson Properties sign; it was their fifth real estate office.

If you google "starting from scratch" you will find the definition: to start from the beginning, to set out on some action or process without prior preparation, knowledge, or advantage. May sound scary, sure, but strong nerve paired with strong faith sends you running to the roar of your lion-sized dream. When you are guided by integrity and have a competitive spirit, you battle through the sleepless nights and find the resilience to juggle the demands of a heavy work load and young family. You keep your head down and keep chasing. You lean on some timely divine intervention, prove the disbelievers wrong, and, one day, you find yourself in the position to pay it forward.

I am honored to write the foreword for Shelly's book, her second lion-sized dream! Because Shelly dared to fail, she is an entrepreneur and author. She has always had a servant's heart and has an encouraging spirit. I know her book will give readers the insight and wisdom to take a chance rather that play it safe.

**Heather J. Brown**
Head Coach, Appalachian State Women's Golf

# INTRODUCTION

# WHY *STARTING FROM SCRATCH?*

**M**ore than a decade ago, my husband Phil and I went to a fundraiser at a private home for Charlotte Mayor Pat McCrory, who later became governor of North Carolina. When we pulled into the gates of the Charlotte neighborhood, I was enamored. It was the most beautiful neighborhood we'd ever been in. The homes were well cared for; the streetlamps cast a wondrous glow over the manicured lawns. I asked Phil, "Do you think we could ever live in a neighborhood like this?" Phil laughed at the question but said, "Maybe; I sure would like to." It was the end of that conversation, but it was just the beginning of a dream.

At the start of our marriage, I made $19,000 a year. We lived in a 1,000 square foot home that cost $55,000 that I purchased the same year we were married. We were happy, but we were also determined at some point to build a business and a life that would allow us more time and flexibility. When it comes to this book, I originally planned to write about parenting. As the mother of two boys (Blake, now twenty-two and Grant, now twenty) I have numerous stories and ideas to share about child-rearing, and raising boys in particular, in our modern culture. As I began writing, however, I realized that I had more to say about growing a family *while* growing a business. In fact, it was difficult for me to separate the two, since I started my family and my business concurrently.

Being a female entrepreneur and a mother has given me a unique perspective on both child-rearing and business building. I believe that my understanding of and appreciation for the interconnectedness of entrepreneurship and family can help you create the work and/or personal life you've always dreamed of. This book is for people in all seasons of life, as everyone starts from scratch at some point: for the young person who wants to start laying the foundation for future successes; for the parent who balances work and home life; for the midlife worker who feels overwhelmed by obligations; for the weary person who needs encouragement; and for the seasoned professional who enjoys the rewards of entrepreneurship. No matter your phase in life or business, this is a book with real emotions and stories that will inspire and encourage you to consider how your values lay the foundation for your success. This book highlights the risks and rewards that go into owning your own business and will illustrate the difficult balance required to raise a family while pursuing professional dreams. The information in these pages will help parents and community leaders mentor the next generation of entrepreneurs and offer practical advice for employees and employers on creating a dynamic atmosphere that is conducive to team and leadership building. By offering some of the same instruction I share in my leadership-training courses, I hope to empower other business leaders to transform their workplaces and their communities. I want everyone to know the pride that comes from building a life to be proud of. I want to help you achieve such a life.

I'm pleased to say that the neighborhood I described above, that once stood as a symbol of possibility and prosperity, is now my neighborhood. Granted, the acquisition of our home was in large part because we knew the market well and got a good price at the right time, but every time I pull up to that gate, I feel both gracious and humbled. To be fair, we're the only house without a pool and, rather than a lawn service, my boys mow our grass; but it doesn't matter. I'm happy to be here. And, quite frankly, I'm *proud* to be here—because I not only dreamed of it, I worked for it.

Henderson Properties began as a hobby in 1990 when Phil started buying real estate as an investment in our future. At the time, people told us we were crazy and tried to talk us out of it. Thankfully, we didn't listen. Fast forward more than two decades—filled with determination, hard work, and a lot of faith—and we own a full-time business with sixty employees. We started our company from scratch—no trust funds, no bank loans. We don't have the perfect marriage, family, or business, but we have unshakable foundations. I hope that this book will help you navigate life's challenges and create a strong base for yourself, your family, and your work peers. When your foundation is strong, you can begin building, from scratch, the life you have always dreamed of.

------------------------------

# CHAPTER 1

# FROM MOM LIFE TO ENTREPRENEURIAL LIFE

*Pour yourself a drink, put on some lipstick, and pull yourself together.*
## — ELIZABETH TAYLOR

**T**he diaper commercials on TV are misleading. They show freshly bathed, happy babies gazing up at well-dressed, cheerful mothers. First-time parents often have the misconception that their baby is going to be totally cute (that part is true), it's going to sleep when they want it to, and will only cry softly at convenient times, at which point they will pick the baby up and it will swiftly nod off to blissful sleep. Nope! That's not the case. The reality is that mom life, like entrepreneurial life, is full of late nights, near disasters, and a lot of messes that only you can clean up. But, oh yeah, it's more than worth it.

In 1998 at the age of thirty-three, I had a three-year-old and an infant, and I had been married to my husband, Phil, for almost seven years. Before our children, I had careers first as a teacher and then as a professional golfer, but at the birth of my eldest son, Blake, I decided to stay home with my children. My motivation was noble, but it didn't prove to be as easy as I'd been led to believe by those distorted TV commercials.

Phil traveled Monday through Thursday for his medical-sales job. It was a job he liked, and he was good at. It afforded us a company car, benefits, and flexibility. I managed the children, the house, and a small number of rental properties we had at the time. Phil had obtained his real estate license before we married and had bought a few fixer-uppers that he rented out. He started doing this three years prior to us getting married, and since we both owned our own homes upon getting married, we had slowly built a nice portfolio.

*As a stay-at-home mom of an infant and toddler, our home was complete chaos.*

As a stay-at-home mom of an infant and toddler, our home was complete chaos. No day was ever the same. Kids got sick, kids cried, kids wanted my attention, kids needed a nap, mom needed a nap. In addition to managing the chaos, I had the other household chores and duties that had to be done each day, mostly as a single parent. Just like any new parent, in my sons' early years, I was just trying to get through the day, trying to appreciate the little things with my little people. I had some family nearby, but they had their own busy working lives, and my friends were in the same parenting chaos as me. Monday was no different than Tuesday, Tuesday was no different than Wednesday, and I found myself getting lost in the mundaneness.

When your children are babies, you live for nap time and dread the witching hours, between the end of naptime and dinner; that's when all hell breaks loose. When every day is like the last, and you have a to-do list that never gets crossed off, it can lead to despair and lack of confidence. Many stay at home parents go from working full time, being surrounded by people, contributing to their family's income to … struggling to find a shirt that doesn't have stains on it. When you're in it, it's hard to see past it. When you're past it, all you want is to be back in it.

Looking back on this time of chaotic early motherhood, I now realize I was undergoing a huge transformation. I was receiving "training" from my new role as mother that would benefit me in the future, both personally and professionally. I was acquiring leadership skills, determination, time-management skills, and persistence. I have always had aspirations, but I haven't always had the confidence and leadership skills to see them through to fruition. This all began to change when I became a parent.

*Looking back on this time of chaotic early motherhood, I now realize I was undergoing a huge transformation. I was receiving "training" from my new role as mother that would benefit me in the future, both personally and professionally.*

My focus and attitude changed with the birth of my children and the subsequent birth of Henderson Properties. Survival of the fittest as they say. Amid the isolation and chaos of early parenting, I was building confidence in my own leadership out of necessity. The mother is the heart of the home. We run the home, whether we work or not. There are some skills we never knew we had until becoming a mother! We are secretaries, bakers, seamstresses, shoppers, planners, nurses, teachers, role models, superheroes. We forgo sleep to hold a sick child all night, and then we do it all over again the next day. It's an intense and challenging period of training and accountability. You can't give up on parenting. You can't fail. If you fail, they fail. Or so we think. You have to "get on the line," as Phil always says, and be the best parent you can be. Everyday. There are no rematches. I think I may have taken this dedication to the extreme, but I was determined not to let these little fellas down. The day my first child was born I remember thinking *Now I get what unconditional love means.* I also felt as though I had been accepted into the "club"— the well-kept secret of care and concern that only a mother knows. It was all very surreal to me in the beginning.

> *You can't give up on parenting. You can't fail. If you fail, they fail. Or so we think. You have to "get on the line," as Phil always says, and be the best parent you can be. Everyday. There are no rematches.*

Phil recently told our youngest son, Grant, "Treat your mother with respect. She would rather have you than me." His words were surprising, but true. Maybe it shouldn't be that way, but it often is. Mother's Day needs to be more than once a year (just saying). Mothers are the warriors, the caretakers, the ones responsible for the well-being of several people. I think all mothers can relate to being leaders. I could be out having dinner with friends, and if my kids needed something, rather than ask their dad sitting next to them on the couch, they'll call me. The phrase, "Go ask your mother" isn't a joke; it's a collective truth. Being a mother can be the most beautiful of burdens.

After the birth of my sons, I realized quickly it wasn't about *me* anymore. It was about these children we'd brought into the world. Their needs came before mine every day, all day. If I didn't take care of them, nobody would. Parenting requires you to be your son's voice, his leader, his advocate. My children have been wonderful teachers for me as well. For example, when my eldest son, Blake, was diagnosed with type 1 diabetes at the age of seven, he looked to me to make it okay; he even asked me once "Will there be diabetes in heaven?" I had to make it okay for him, and there was no other job more important to me. I have always thought of myself as being too nice, but my son's diagnosis challenged me to become an assertive advocate for his health. And I was. With each quarterly doctor visit and health challenge, I grew more and more confident in the mother I wanted to be, in the woman I was becoming, and, though I hadn't fully realized it at the time, in the entrepreneur I was becoming.

> *With each quarterly doctor visit and health challenge, I grew more and more confident in the mother I wanted to be, in the woman I was becoming, and, though I hadn't fully realized it at the time, in the entrepreneur I was becoming.*

Growing my family and my business are intertwined for me. As much as I loved being at home with my boys, I didn't feel completely fulfilled. Mothering was my top priority, but I felt like there was something else I could be doing to help our family. I didn't know what it was. I felt called to make a difference, but I didn't quite know how to do that. I felt pulled in several directions, and I didn't know how to reconcile my inner drive with my family's needs. At that time, we weren't actively trying to grow our property-management business. We were, however, trying to figure out a way for me to work without spending all our income on day care.

"I want to do *something*," I'd say to Phil.

"What do you want to do?" Phil would ask.

"I don't know."

"What are you good at?"

"I DON'T KNOW WHAT I'M GOOD AT! I'M A STAY-AT-HOME MOM!"

We had this conversation repeatedly. After we became parents, our priorities organically shifted. We were focused on our family and wanted to provide them a quality future without sacrificing flexible schedules. I think starting a family was a good reprieve for us; it enabled us to take a step back and say, *What's next?* We began thinking about the bigger picture, about our legacy. We ruminated for a while, and then one day, after we had acquired several more properties to manage, we realized we were looking to *start* a business when we already *had* a business that was expanding right before our eyes.

That's not to say that things got easier from then on. After we decided to cultivate our property-management company, it was still total chaos. In the '90s, we didn't have the benefit of technology to keep us efficient and organized. We didn't have voice mail, text messaging, or e-mail. If you wanted to talk to somebody, you had to call them on their landline, and if he or she wasn't there, you left a message on an answering machine. Our phone rang constantly. Tenants called because their dishwasher broke; they had an electrical issue; they had a question about their rent; they inquired about a rental ad we'd placed in the newspaper.

When Phil would leave on Monday morning for his four-day business trip each week, he would say, "Don't answer the phone if the kids are crying." One week, he came home and asked, "Why do we have fifty-five messages on the answering machine?" I responded, "You said not to answer the phone when the kids were crying. Well, they cried the whole time!"

I was the one showing rental properties to prospective tenants. When we would get a phone call from someone wanting to see a property, I'd have to map out my route (using an actual map!) before I got in the car; if prospective tenants were unable to keep our appointment, there was no way for them to reach me once I left the house. I'd pile a toddler and a baby in the car at naptime and go to various rental properties. I'd show the houses and hurry people along, because I had two sleeping kids in the car, and I was trying to do it all within the two hours that I had. If the kids were awake, I had no choice but to bring them in with me, and they would run around the house while I showed the property. It wasn't until a little later in our careers that we could afford child care.

There was a lot of chaos, but it was good chaos. It was our chaos, and I treasured it. Dealing with that chaos was overwhelming, as there were little resources available to support our business endeavors. To add to the mania, when we went full time with Henderson Properties, we had little money to live on. We survived that first year of the business on about $18,000 with two children who were in diapers. But in many ways, it was the best of times, because we were together. We had this little family, and if we wanted to get out, we put the kids in the wagon and walked to the local Dairy Queen for ice cream. Sometimes friends would give us extra Charlotte Hornets tickets, and that would be our entertainment. We were happy and grateful.

I'm often asked if I was scared when we started the company, but I wasn't. We had a vision, we had goals, we had a purpose, and as Phil says, we had the "want to." Fortunately for us, our children were also young enough that if we failed, they wouldn't remember. We also had youth on our side: I was thirty-three, and Phil was thirty-five. We figured if we gave it a few years and it didn't work out, he would still be young enough to start a new career or go back to his sales job. I could return to teaching. My confidence level in some ways went up during this time, because it *had* to. I knew what the successful journey looked like, but I didn't know what the unsuccessful journey looked like. That was my motivation.

*We had a vision, we had goals, we had a purpose, and as Phil says, we had the "want to." Fortunately for us, our children were also young enough that if we failed, they wouldn't remember.*

I'm not interested in misleading entrepreneurial women like I was misled by diaper commercials with beautiful babies and calm mothers. It's hard. Real hard. Time management and finding a proper balance is never easy, you just get more skilled at it. When people had an emergency at their property, and my child was crying, I had to choose. My children are my top priority, but I also have an obligation to other people, as well. My children were somewhat predictable, but sometimes the unpredictable happened, and an

*I'm not interested in misleading entrepreneurial women like I was misled by diaper commercials with beautiful babies and calm mothers. It's hard. Real hard.*

employee wouldn't show up for work, or I had an emergency at a rental property, and that would have to take precedence.

The whole thing about an "ideal" work/life balance is that the ratio shifts daily. It has to. There are times when everything is great, and your life is calm, and then all hell breaks loose, and you have to divert your attention to the immediate need. There are some things that a mom entrepreneur is going to have to expect—like the unexpected! You're always going to struggle with time management and who comes first. You're just going to have to pick and choose who or what needs the most attention at a particular time.

You're also going to experience guilt. It's inevitable and it's debilitating if you let it be, and it won't go away until you prove your success to yourself; then you can justify that it was all worth it. But in the moment, get consumed with your current task and let yourself feel that innate will to survive and succeed. It's the antidote to mom-guilt. I often felt guilty, as many mothers do: guilty if you do it, guilty if you don't do it. My challenge was to figure out what would fulfill me and how I could make it happen, while keeping my family as my top priority. Sometimes that meant that my children spent time at day care. Sometimes that meant they watched TV. Sometimes that meant we ate Chick-fil-A for dinner.

I don't feel guilty about any of that today. In fact, I wish I hadn't wasted so much time and energy feeling bad. I was working hard to make my children's futures as bright as they could be. That's something I wish I'd been more focused on when they were young. Mothers do what they

> *I don't feel guilty about any of that today. In fact, I wish I hadn't wasted so much time and energy feeling bad.*

need to do *now* so that their children can have a nice life *later*. For example, sometimes I felt guilty about putting my children in day care, but I needed them to be in a safe environment that was away from our home office for an extended period of time to free up my time to build a business. And that was okay. In fact, I would have much more guilt now if we had not taken the risk to become entrepreneurs. The risks outweighed the rewards at that time and it wasn't worth the energy it took to feel guilty.

Entrepreneurship can mean different things for different women. You don't have to own your own business. You could be the head of a corporation, or be part of the management team that runs a small business. Moms need to give themselves more grace. I think I tried so hard to be "Wonder Woman" that a lot of the time I felt like a failure. Women in leadership must show grace to themselves and other women. It's really okay if you go through the drive-thru for dinner. The kids survive. The wheel still turns, life moves on, everybody's still happy if dinner isn't home cooked. You've got to take it one day at a time, because no day is the same as the next day, and if you don't do it, then nobody else will. You must capitalize on opportunities when you have them. If you have an opportunity to take a CEO position, or buy a franchise corporation, or work hard in a multi-tier business, you shouldn't say *no* just because you're a mom with household responsibilities. In fact, being a mom might be the reason you have a competitive edge. Our families can still come first, but not at the expense of ourselves and our

> *You shouldn't say no just because you're a mom with household responsibilities. In fact, being a mom might be the reason you have a competitive edge.*

entrepreneurial spirits. I am all about the opportunity so to speak. Don't let it pass you by.

Sometimes the most challenging aspect of growing as a mother and entrepreneur is your thought patterns. I had to foster the mind-set that nothing is ever a problem—not my never-ending to-do list, and certainly not my children. Going from mom life to entrepreneurial life means rising above the chaotic *now* and seeing your family's bright future. It also means taking ownership and satisfaction from being an integral part of that success.

When we started our business, our goal was to be all-in. When we started Henderson Properties, I remember Phil asking me, "Are you in this 110 percent?" And my answer was, "Absolutely. I'm in it; you're in it; we're in it to win it!"

---

## HENDERSON PROPERTIES EMPLOYEE SPOTLIGHT:

*I just want to say how grateful I am to be working for Henderson Properties and how you have developed a company that has such a feeling of family. In this fast-paced world, we don't always take the time to stop and say thank you, and I want to take this time to say that to both of you. Thank you for choosing me to be a part of the Henderson Properties family.*

**TAMRA GOODMAN**

*Community Association Manager*

---

# CHAPTER 2

-----------------------------------

# STARTING FROM SCRATCH

*I didn't get there by wishing for it or hoping for it, but by working for it.*

**— ESTEE LAUDER**

There are some moments in life you remember more vividly than others. On September 16, 1998, after three years of managing properties for other people and growing our own rental portfolio with homes we obtained through short sales, foreclosures, or relocating friends, my husband and I decided to become full time entrepreneurs.

Phil had been working as a medical salesman, a job that he loved; but on this day, he called his manager and gave his notice that he would be leaving to start our own business. I remember standing in the kitchen with our two young sons playing at my feet when Phil came downstairs, looked at me, and said, "Well, I did it. Now what?"

*Now what!* I tried to hide my panic. What had we done? Saying I was all-in was one thing, actually making it happen was another. Phil loved his job; he drove a company car; he had health-care benefits; he made a good salary. He just gave it all up. Phil must have sensed my hesitation because he quickly added, "Whatever happens, we're in it together. We'll just see what happens, but we've got to give it a try." It was true. And when I glanced at our two young boys at my feet, I realized we could provide them a good life and positive leadership examples, if we could make this work.

Despite my initial fear, it felt right to take a leap at that specific time. Plus, I felt as though entrepreneurship was in my blood. My father was an entrepreneur. My mother's father tried his hand as an entrepreneur. My mother's brother and his sons are entrepreneurs. I felt the calling to be my own boss and to create my own destiny, despite the risks involved. As for Phil, he had the schooling background with a business administration degree, and he also had the sales background, winning several awards at the company he worked for. I had been a golf professional, a teacher, and a stay-at-home mom. We would learn over the years that our personal endeavors, though varied, had created an ideal environment for us to learn important skills that would benefit us as entrepreneurs.

----------------------------

*We would learn over the years that our personal endeavors, though varied, had created an ideal environment for us to learn important skills that would benefit us as entrepreneurs.*

----------------------------

Despite Phil's educational background, we quickly realized that entrepreneurship is like parenting: you can read all the books you can get your hands on, but at the end of the day, you don't really know the situation until you live it. One of the first things we had to teach ourselves about business, was that being nice didn't get you far. We had to toughen up a bit. Being a nice, Southern gentlewoman didn't guarantee that people were going to treat you the same way. We had to learn the right balance between head and heart.

We also had to teach ourselves the rules and regulations of property management. Even though Phil had his North Carolina real estate broker license, we still had to make sure we fully understood all policies and procedures. For example, after committing fully to Henderson Properties, we had to evict a tenant who never took her things out of the small one-bedroom apartment she lived in. After a few weeks asking her (nicely!) to get her things out and even after she left the premises, she still refused, so we took a truckload of junk and threw it away. Time is money. She decided to take us to court and won—because, apparently, we didn't go through the proper chain of command to evict her; we ended up having to compensate her for $2,000 worth of personal items she left behind, even though she owed us $800 in back rent. Lesson learned.

Afterwards, we decided to follow procedures down to the smallest detail in order to build a reputation that matched our values. Since then, the Charlotte judicial system tends to favor us, because our property managers come prepared and armed with documentation and photos. We pride ourselves on adherence to the rules and regulations. Not only did we strengthen our people skills and learn the laws of property management, we also had to understand in what direction to take the company.

I don't believe that one sets out to be a real estate entrepreneur and says, "Okay, first we're going to have the rental properties, and then we're going to have the employees, and then we're going to add the maintenance department." Sometimes it's not what you *want*, but what you *need*. We taught ourselves how to make strategic decisions based on what was necessary, not what we necessarily wanted. One of the greatest challenges of early entrepreneurship is not having a handbook to follow. When we started Henderson Properties, it was up to Phil and me to decide how it would be run, and each of those decisions determined whether or not it would be sustainable and successful.

We started this venture with enough money in our savings account to sustain us for about four or five months. We knew, because we didn't take out a loan, that the pressure was on. I was not working, because I was at home with the children full time. We understood completely that if we were successful, it was on us. If we were unsuccessful, it was also on us. So, we were determined to make it. There was no turning back. The first six months of our business was a lean time. We didn't spend much money on anything other than groceries and diapers. It's amazing that when you don't have anything, you may actually feel like you have more than you need—or at least enough to sustain you. What we did have was each other's support. We became our own CEOs. I had trust and faith in my husband and our partnership. When you have to rely on somebody more than yourself, it adds value to your relationship and teamwork. We never thought of what we were going through as a rough time. Some days were challenging, but we knew that if we could get through that first pivotal year, we might be able to make Henderson Properties work.

Being in partnership with an athlete became a huge asset at

> *We never thought of what we were going through as a rough time. Some days were challenging, but we knew that if we could get through that first pivotal year, we might be able to make Henderson Properties work.*

this point in our lives. Phil and I both attended Appalachian State University. I was on a golf scholarship, and he was a walk-on for the football team. Athletes know how to persevere; otherwise they don't do well on the field. I believe being part of teams in our formative years helped us to rely on each other and not accept failure. One reason I feel so strongly about sports is that there's something about being on a team that makes you mindful of there not being an "I" in team. It is a collective group with the same goals working together in unity. I think that's probably why

*Athletes know how to persevere; otherwise they don't do well on the field. I believe being part of teams in our formative years helped us to rely on each other and not accept failure.*

we never discussed what would happen if we didn't make it. We just assumed we *would* make it. Phil would always yell "Get on the line!" at football games when the offensive line was too slow coming out of the huddle for the next play. It became a joke in our house. Amid all our chaos with young children and an equally young business, we'd use the phrase to hurry the kids along or to get our heads in the game when our entrepreneurial confidence was waning. Corny but we had to have some humor to get us through.

During our early years, we set out as a property management company and we focused on obtaining new clients and making sure we maintained current ones. When you're starting out with twenty clients, and you lose one, that's a huge loss. Every week, Phil opened the Yellow Pages and cold-called every real estate company in Charlotte and the surrounding areas, asking the broker-in-charge if any property management services, which were not popular, were needed. If so, he graciously asked if he could speak at their next staff meeting and tell them what Henderson Properties had to offer.

In the beginning, that's how we developed leads. It was either by word of mouth or picking up the phone and calling somebody and asking, "Do you need our services? Would you like to hear about our services?" And we were confident that if we could get Phil in the door, they would not turn him away. The business didn't grow itself. We worked for each and every client we had. Then we'd work just as hard to keep that client.

In becoming an entrepreneur, you're thrown into a leadership role. Phil was not only the leader of our family, he was also the leader of our business; my role was co-leader of the business and leader of the home. It wasn't always easy to distinguish these roles. Working with your spouse from home with two young children is quite challenging. Phil had his mission for the day, his goals, his to-do lists; I had mine.

*The business didn't grow itself. We worked for each and every client we had. Then we'd work just as hard to keep that client.*

Sometimes our goals for the day clashed. If he needed to make twenty calls, and I needed the kids to be able to run and yell and get some energy out, that didn't always turn out well. Phil was focused on work; I was focused on work and home. It was tough to determine which of our daily goals took priority. In the beginning, we did not tag team as well as we could've. Most of the responsibilities fell to me. It was what I agreed to. Nobody was forcing me. However, there were days when it was overwhelming, and I felt alone—or felt some resentment toward Phil. The days were going by so fast with the boys, all the while, we were trying to grow the business.

All these issues came to a head as you can imagine fairly quickly. Henderson Properties had been full time for about three months. Our younger son, Grant, who was eleven months old at the time, had to go to the doctor because a growth had literally popped up on his neck. After the doctor treated him for a few days with no improvement, he told us he was admitting Grant to the hospital, because there was nothing more he could do. I was a wreck. When I called Phil to tell him, he said, "You just go on to the hospital, and I'll meet you when the office closes." My response to him was calm but direct: "If you're going to wait, then I suggest you not come at all." He got the hint and wrapped things up to meet us at the hospital.

I did feel like, a lot of the time, I oversaw a lot of business things by myself, and I made decisions for our children by myself. In hindsight, however, this time made me much more independent. I didn't rely on Phil or anybody else to make the decisions. It was a transformative period for me because I not only had to take care of these two children, but I had a husband and a business to take care of. Not every day was challenging, but there were several times when I thought being both Phil's wife and his business partner wasn't viable.

In July 1999, we had been running the business full time for ten months. We were both cementing our roles within the company and figuring out how to work together out of the house. At this point, we had a four-year-old and an eighteen-month-old, so our 1,700 square foot home was louder and more crammed than ever before. Having our offices at home was becoming problematic. It was hard to answer our phones in the midst of our children's chaos, but when people have a problem with their home or they want to see a manager, they need to talk to a person, and they want to talk immediately, not tomorrow, not in two days. When you're in the property-management business, the phone doesn't stop ringing at five o'clock p.m. We advertised our rental properties in the newspaper, and people would read our ads at night after work. So, we had calls at eight o'clock at night; we had calls at eight o'clock in the morning. We had repair calls at various times of the day, so the chaos finally took its toll and one day I looked at Phil and said, "Something has to go. It's either you or the business." As you can imagine, shortly thereafter, we were able to acquire a one-room office away from the clamor of home. This allowed Phil and me to focus on work when we were at the office, and on our family when we were at home.

*During our growth, it was challenging to learn how to do everything that was needed, do it well, and then know when outside help was needed.*

During our growth, it was challenging to learn how to do everything that was needed, do it well, and then know when outside help was needed. How do we hire the right people? Do we take a paycheck? Do we not take a paycheck? How much money do we keep in the business? Which bill do we pay first? Do we hire a full-time employee? If we do, what do we pay that person? Certainly, we had to take care of our family first, but how do you take care of your family without generating an income? It was such a balancing act, deciding what we should do and when we should do it. So many questions, so little time!

As the first year progressed, we had a separate office space, and we were able to generate a little income. By then our savings were depleted, so we were relying strictly on the business to generate revenue. We needed to brand ourselves with a name and a logo. We wanted to keep our last name as part of the business, because we thought that would help hold us accountable and perhaps encourage us to try a little bit harder to succeed. Our name was literally on the line, as was our reputation. We relied on some friends to lend us their expertise in those early years. One friend was kind enough to lend us her graphic-arts expertise, and she designed the logo that we still use today. It was important to us that we keep that logo through the years, though we have rebranded, as necessary, by adding other real estate services to our business.

We had many firsts that year: our first office space, our first logo, our first employees. We also experienced other firsts that were much more difficult: firing our first employee and having our first tenants who were unable to pay rent. Firing somebody is never easy and never *will* be easy. Wondering what to do next is never easy. To this day, people in the office still laugh because they think Phil is a "ponderer," and they say he takes too long to make a decision. Time is crucial when the decision affects the good of the group. The balance is always between the risk vs. reward.

As we progressed through the first year and into the second, we had doubled our portfolio. We started with managing twenty properties, but then we were up to fifty-five properties. Our business continued to be profitable. We continued to get leads. Phil continued to generate friendships in the community and the real estate industry, whether it was with the cold calls, the continuing education classes he took for his real estate license, or the advertisements and word-of-mouth references.

We slowly built a reputation in the Charlotte area as a property-management company. Fortunately, that reputation has stayed with us, and now that we are a full-service real estate firm, it's been an ongoing process to rebrand ourselves. To date, we're much more than that, and we are proud to offer—in addition to property management—maintenance, accounting, homeowner-association management, and real estate sales services. Someone could rent a property from us, then decide to buy a property from us, and then need to maintain that property. We can handle all of that. We can help with everything that has to do with an existing home, whether it's the maintenance, the purchase of the home, the selling of the home, or the managing of the home. Every service added, every employee gained, every office-space expansion has been lovingly and painstakingly built from scratch. We worked and learned and loved during the entire process, and that is what makes Henderson Properties so unique.

## "GET ON THE LINE"

### by Phil Henderson

I'm often asked about the moment Shelly and I made the leap into entrepreneurship. For some people, it's a gradual process. For us, it was a conscious decision that changed our lives in an instant. Before I even submitted my resignation to my medical-sales job, I had been thinking a lot about how the decision would affect me and my family. Up to that point, I had always worked for another corporation. I had always depended on the weekly paycheck that my employer provided. I had grown to enjoy the benefits of working for someone else—health insurance, paid vacation days, paid sick leave, and a corporate expense account for meals and lodging. In addition, the company I worked for, Wilson-Cook Medical, had an annual sales meeting at exclusive resorts where I could bring Shelly along with me. I knew I would miss all of that, but I knew I'd especially miss my company car. I had utilized a company car for the last twelve years and never bought any gasoline or paid for any maintenance or auto insurance. Should I really give up all this security?

As I debated resigning, I wondered how we would be able to replace all those benefits. I had to secure health insurance for my young family. I had to buy a vehicle to use for our emerging business. All these changes and challenges brought on both fear and excitement. Where would the money come from? How would we afford health insurance? What happens if the kids get sick? These fears were running through my mind on an hourly basis.

The biggest fear that I had to face, however, was the fear of failure. What happens if we don't make this new business a success? How can I face my wife and tell her we failed and I'm going to have to try to find a new job? How could I face the people who said we were crazy to walk away from a salary to start this business? How could I face my friends and tell them that I just wasn't good enough to make it in business?

Fear can be a powerful motivator. Those fears of letting Shelly and my boys down fueled my determination to work hard and ensure that I didn't have to have those tough conversations about failure. There were many things that motivated me in those early months of starting Henderson Properties, but the biggest motivation was that I knew Shelly, Blake, and Grant were counting on me, and I wasn't going to let them down.

While Shelly took care of the phones and the administrative tasks, I worked long hours making cold calls to the office managers or sales managers of all real estate brokerage firms in the greater Charlotte area. I tried to convince them to allow me to come to their Realtor sales meetings so that I could educate them on our property-management services. Most Realtors at that time did not want to have anything to do with property management but needed someone to refer their investor clients to when they had a need for property management. I wanted to be the "go-to" property-management company for all the Realtors in the greater Charlotte area.

As I did more and more sales presentations to the real estate brokerage offices, I realized that there was a real need for a quality property-management firm in the greater Charlotte area. Up to that point, there were only one or two firms that were providing quality services. The rest of the firms in existence were mainly small firms that only provided a basic level of service.

Learning more about the strong demand for our services and more about our competition showed me that if we were going to be successful, we had to do it by offering superior services. To do that, we had to have quality people and cutting-edge technology.

That early understanding of the industry and competition convinced me that our company had to be different. I'm proud to say that Henderson Properties is unique in the Charlotte market. We are the only real estate-service firm that provides four services under one roof: rental-property management, community-association management, real estate-brokerage and maintenance/renovations services. We are the "one-stop shop" for real estate investors, community association boards of directors, and buyers and sellers of real estate.

There are two other things that make Henderson Properties unique. The first is our people—our staff of rental-property managers and community-association managers are all experienced with an average of more than six years in the industry. The property-management industry typically has frequent turnover; because of the culture at Henderson Properties and the work/life balance we promote, however, we've had above-average tenure in both of these critical customer-contact positions.

The other thing that makes Henderson Properties unique is our technology. We utilize industry-leading technology in our sales-brokerage division, rental-property-management division, and our community-association-management division. This technology allows our clients to access information about their accounts online all day, every day.

I will never say it was an easy choice to take the leap from being a salaried employee to an entrepreneur, but I will always say that it was the right choice. During my years playing football, I came to appreciate the coach's demand to "get on the line." It was often used when there was no time to think. Just get in your position, do what you do best, and make your team proud. For me, 1998 was when I "got on the line." I didn't think, I just trusted my position, my skill set, and my teammate, Shelly. When an opportunity presents itself, you must be willing to take the risk; otherwise there is no chance of a reward.

-----------------------------------------------------

## HENDERSON PROPERTIES EMPLOYEE SPOTLIGHT:

*Finding a balance between home and work life is difficult. I believe one of the reasons people in my field—community association managers—get burned out and end up switching careers is all of the night meetings. It is great that Henderson Properties values the work/life balance. I have seen Phil fight hard to get boards to move their monthly meetings to daytime hours. In fact, if boards do not comply, there is an extra charge. This really helps keep us from sitting in a clubhouse until eleven o'clock p.m. instead of being with our families. It's one of the many ways Henderson Properties tries to help employees balance our work lives and our home lives.*

**MATT PRYOR**

*Community Association Manager*

----------------------------------------------------------

# CHAPTER 3

------------------------------

# BUILDING YOUR TEAM

*A kid grows up a lot faster on the golf course.*
*Golf teaches you how to behave.*
**— JACK NICKLAUS**

ine hundred-ninety-seven, *swing*
Nine-hundred-ninety-eight, *swing,*
Nine-hundred-ninety-nine, *swing,*
One thousand, *swing.*

When I was eleven, my father decided I should play golf. My earliest golf memories include getting up each summer morning and heading to the driving range to hit one thousand balls. My father thought of that number, not me. There I would stay for the four hours it took, counting each and every ball. Then usually I played afterwards or had a lesson. I didn't want to disappoint my parents, and though I sometimes didn't want to spend my summers hitting golf balls, it became a habit I grew to enjoy. I never understood why my golf training was so important to my father. I guess he decided it would either keep me out of trouble or pay my way through college. Either way, it managed to do both. I think he was also hoping I might be the next Nancy Lopez (young people may need to google her), though that wasn't my goal. I didn't have the desire then. Or maybe it was that I didn't have the right coaching I needed by my father; either way I did treat it as my summer job though, and usually played most of the day. I did it to the best of my ability and was held accountable by my father. There were a lot of expectations. If my father had been more of a coach, mentor, or engaged father, maybe I would've taken the sport more seriously and my path might have changed. The only thing my father ever wanted to talk about with me was golf: if I played, how I'd played, how many balls I hit. I started to believe that if I played well, my father loved me; if I didn't play well, he didn't love me. I became a little jaded, and this dynamic affected my view of golf and my self esteem for a long time. Despite the hundreds of hours I spent playing each summer, it still didn't feel like the game belonged to me.

Between fifth and twelfth grades, I played in summer tournaments both in and out of town and was on the boys' golf teams in both middle and high school. Being part of a male team helped me later in life to relate to both sexes. It was this early experience on a boys' team that allows me to fill in for Phil with any group, even a men's business group, with confidence and ease. Growing up in a boys' atmosphere gave me an edge that I am so appreciative of. I had to have conversations with these boys. I had to play against them. Some of them I beat, some of them beat me. The term "girls rule" didn't apply back then. The boys were always fair and polite and probably a little impressed if I won the match. I never experienced a situation where any of us were better than the rest.

Because I was practicing seven days a week at this point, I became pretty good. Practice makes perfect, right? My parents decided I should play on the women's league at the country club to challenge me more. This was a pivotal moment: I was sixteen years old and was given the opportunity to play with women much older than myself who had decades of golf experience. This should have been a mentoring opportunity for these women, but that's not what happened. Instead the women felt extremely threatened by my youth and my skill, and instead of being accepting and stepping up as potential role models for me, they tried to bring me down.

I have clear memories of some of these women being extremely nasty and rude to my mother and me. It was ridiculous that all this negativity took place over one young girl wanting to be a part of the women's group. Even I could see it. At that time I learned what team building truly meant. Even at my young age of sixteen, I rec-

> *At that moment I learned what team building truly meant.*

ognized that these women were afraid to play with somebody who was better than them. Or maybe it was that I was younger. Let me reiterate that they weren't playing for anything but a win or a title as the club champion. As I got older, I understood how intimidating this can be. Once I got into the business world, I was reminded of these women and their fear. Today it is called bullying and surely would not be tolerated. Maybe golf was all those women had to empower them. I think about that now as I'm writing this book and I pity them for not being able to rise above and do the right thing by accepting this young girl into their midst. If you live your life in fear, you can't be positive. There's no way you could be a positive person, and there isn't a lot of room for success—in life, in business, in family—if you're a negative person. I was determined that in my future I would find people who would help support me and build me up. I would find "my team." I was also inspired to create a future for myself that would allow me opportunities to mentor young women about team building and leadership from a place of love and support, not fear and jealousy. This is one reason I became a teacher. Because of this early experience, a line was drawn in the sand. Some ladies would play with me, others would not. Some stayed friends with my mother, others did not. Some of their husbands wanted to duke it out with my father in the parking lot. Seriously! Today I can say *oh well*, but back then, I'll admit that being a teenager was hard enough; dealing with this was harder but thankfully short lived. There ended up being a truce and I like to think that my mother and I were instrumental in paving the way for other young female golfers to have a chance to play at any level in the private country club sector.

At that point, I was a practiced, seasoned golfer, and my parents and I began looking at various schools where I could continue my golf career. My dream would have been to go to Wake Forest University and play on their golf team, but I didn't try hard to go there. I didn't even apply because I didn't have the confidence that I do now. So, I looked at other schools. When I visited Appalachian State University (ASU), I fell in love. It's unique, being in the North Carolina mountains. It's beautiful and has four distinct seasons. The leaves are magical in the fall, and it snows there. It was only two hours from home. I loved it. I never looked back. Today it is still affectionately known as my "happy place."

## TEAM BUILDING IN SPORTS

ASU offered me a full golf scholarship, and I accepted. I started collegiate golf in the fall of 1983. I began to realize how sheltered I'd been at home. I didn't have a lot of responsibility at the time other than school and golf. My father wouldn't allow me to get a job, because he felt like golf was my job. In essence it was and it met a goal which was to play at the next level. But at the next level I didn't really understand what it meant to be accountable to other people. That first semester was a difficult transition. I had teammates. I had a roommate. I was in a new town. I was now accountable to all these different people and schedules. At eighteen years old, I found myself in this tornado of responsibility that I had never experienced before. I felt out of place. I wasn't quite sure where I fit in. Furthermore, my golf team had a lot of upheaval that first year, and we were lacking the team unity that would have benefited me.

As I progressed in college, my golf team became more cohesive because the ones not committed dropped out and the ones who were there for the right reasons rose to the occasion. This helped me overall with my sense of belonging and my confidence. In some ways it was the support system that got me through the rough time that followed. So much of my golf training was still tied up in my dad's expectations of me. During this time, when I

> *As I progressed in college, my golf team became more cohesive, and it helped me overall with my sense of belonging and my con-fidence. In some ways it was the support system that got me through the rough time that followed.*

was nineteen years old, my parents separated, ultimately divorcing a few years later ... I felt isolated and alone primarily because I didn't know anyone else who's parents had divorced. This was a big setback for my confidence; however, this was when I realized that every circumstance and obstacle pushes you to the next step on the path. I was at the fork in the road, and I knew that I had to choose— go the right path or the wrong path. I chose the right path. From that time forward, I wanted to be the change for myself and those around me. That same year, my sophomore year, I was named most valuable player of my team. This was a pivotal moment that helped restore some of the confidence I had lost with my parents' divorce. I also decided to join a sorority—one with no reputation because it was new to campus. I look back fondly on that sophomore year in college. For some reason, I was courageous enough to try something new and brave enough not to give up on the game that I had grown to love. Two circumstances at such a young age changed the course of my life. As fate would have it, it was also the same year I started dating my future husband. Little did I know at that time how fateful that year would prove to be.

The summer after my junior year, I was playing in the North Carolina Women's Amateur golf tournament in Asheville NC, and I set a record. I shot sixty-nine, with a thirty-nine on the front and a thirty on the back nine, which included six birdies in those nine holes. I didn't win the tournament, but according to *Golf Digest*, I did set a record with six birdies in nine holes. In my heart, though, I had won something more. That was a turning point for me. Golf suddenly felt like it was *mine.* It was no longer my father's sport. Though it was a sad time in my home life, there was a lot of empowerment I felt as well. It felt good to be successful on my own merit and to enjoy something I excelled at. I began to understand the importance of not only team building but my place on the team. I understood what it meant to belong.

When my father left my family, it was the hardest thing imaginable at my young age. Luckily, I had the support of my team, a few of whom I'm still close with. This was one of my earliest lessons in the importance of surrounding myself with the right kind of teammates. It's not just important, it's essential. When you are part of a team, whether it's high school, college, or the working world, everybody claims his or her spot on the team. On our golf team, the older girls were the leaders of the team. It was a hierarchy. Of course, the team changed each year as girls graduated and new girls joined. We had coaching challenges too. In the '80s, women's sports weren't taken too seriously, so our coach was part-time. I had two different coaches in four years, and because of this, my team had to become united and make sure we held ourselves and each other accountable. Though it wasn't the ideal leadership dynamic, it did force us young women athletes to figure things out, prioritize, and strengthen our time-management skills. I am a better leader today, because I had good peer role models on my golf team. When one graduated, another took her place. The team dynamic would shift, but the values of the team—the support, the positivity, the drive—would remain. There was no drama, only camaraderie. But that could be because of the smallness of the group and there weren't too many personalities to deal with. Being part of a smaller team has a lot of advantages, because you're forced to claim your spot. If you're not pulling your weight, it's very noticeable.

Sports training helped prepare me for being an entrepreneur, because I had to find my place on the team and ways to better the team. Golf is such a gentle sport. It taught me to be gracious and responsible. Time management was key with practice, tee times, and getting in eighteen holes in a timely manner. It taught me how to manage my disappointment, because not every day on the golf course is a good day, just like not every day at work is a good day. I'm partial to golfers, because not only are they playing for their team, but they're also playing for themselves as individuals. Golf is often a solitary game, in that you can't talk to your team members much when you're on the course, but you all keep the same goal in mind. These were important lessons to understand early in my life, and they've served me well in business and marriage. I began to understand how important it is to build your personal and professional team consciously, making certain you are choosing to surround yourself with people who want you to succeed.

## TEAM BUILDING IN LIFE

My pastor, David Chadwick of Forest Hill Church, said the two things that will direct your life are the books you read and the person you choose to marry. I can attest to that! One of my most pivotal team-building experiences happened off the course. Of course, I didn't know it at the time, but meeting Phil and ultimately choosing him as my teammate, my spouse, my business partner, was one of the most important decisions of my life.

Phil and I met in college. I was a freshman and he was a junior. We were introduced in the cafeteria by a mutual friend; my roommate. We had one date, which went well, but we were both busy and distracted and went our separate ways. My golf team had two seasons, the fall and the spring, and we traveled both seasons. Because of my golf schedule, it was rare for me to attend all home football games, but I was able to go to one my sophomore year, and as fate would have it, I crossed paths again with Phil at halftime. We stopped and chatted for a minute, and he asked me out again. I agreed, and we made plans for the following week.

When he came to pick me up outside my dorm, he was on a motorcycle. As he handed me a helmet, my first thought was, *My mother is not going to like this.* We went to a place in Boone and had a wonderful time. Despite my hesitation about the motorcycle, we proceeded to date for the next three years. Phil and I were so different when we dated. I didn't know at the time that this would be in our favor later in life. We had come from such different backgrounds. I was born the oldest of two sisters in the suburbs of Detroit until I was in the fourth grade and moved to Charlotte. Phil was from a rural town in North Carolina and was an only child. I was a Catholic girl; he was a Southern Baptist. Phil took risks; I was a rule follower, a people pleaser. Phil graduated college that next year; I was still in school. When I graduated, we were at that crossroads where we decided we should either get married or break up. We broke up, and I was heartbroken.

After graduation, I returned to Charlotte. I still thought about him often, but I was focused on my new teaching career and figuring out life after college. We had no contact after breaking up. Eighteen months went by, and on the way home from visiting a friend in the area, I stopped by to say hello to his parents. They asked me if I ever talked to Phil, and I said no. Keep in mind, there was no Facebook, there were no cell phones. If you ended a relationship, there was no way to "change your status" or try to keep track of someone. To get in touch with someone, you had to call on a landline or you had to write a letter. Phil's parents informed me that Phil had bought a house in Charlotte, and they gave me his phone number. Four months went by before I worked up the courage to call him. He seemed happy to hear from me. He said he was going

*We dated another two and a half years before getting married in 1991. Not even realizing I had begun building my team, and I couldn't have been happier with my choice.*

out of town but would call me the following week. He kept his promise and called. We dated another two and a half years before getting married in 1991. Not even realizing I had begun building my team, and I couldn't have been happier with my choice.

As I write these words, Phil and I have been married for twenty-six years, and during that time, we have called on our sports training to aid our partnership numerous times. For the first ten years of Henderson Properties, Phil and I worked side-by-side at home and at the job. Despite its challenges, this dynamic strengthened our relationship. We each grew into the team player the other one needed. We also gained mutual respect because of the dedication and perseverance we saw in one another. Though we hadn't planned on this personal reward, I think Phil and I have a stronger partnership and marriage because of our time and dedication to Henderson Properties. This bond will forever stay with us and trickle down to our children. We understand the importance of balancing self and the team. It has been a bit more of give and take because we are so different, but different is good. I now take more risks and step outside the box because of him. He pushes me to complete tasks and become organized. You know how some people have good intentions, but active steps are never taken? That doesn't happen in my house. Phil will make it happen. He is a man of his word. I appreciate that so much. We understand the value of having shared goals. We recognize that a positive attitude can save even the most challenging of days.

We have taken the team-building lessons we learned in sports and applied them to our marriage and to our parenting. When we had our two sons, we felt like we were growing in all aspects. We are their first coaches, and I'm proud of who they have become. They have the confidence and the drive that I'm not sure I had at their ages. Blake, who was diagnosed at age seven with type 1 diabetes, never let that limit him. He went to college with an opportunity to play football and is now a leader in his fraternity. Few people know what a child or parent of a type 1 diabetic must deal with every day, but what happens to one person on your team, happens to all. Little brother Grant became an advocate too. Diabetes has brought our family closer together. I didn't see it then, but I realize it now. With Blake's diagnosis, we had to dig deep in our athletic training and positivity to get through it. Every day in the beginning was a huge challenge. I feel confident that one of the reasons Blake believed in himself is because he had a good team—his family. We want to build the boys up while also maintaining healthy limits. With both our children, we try to be the mentors, the team leaders, that we needed at their ages. We know how valuable the lessons they're learning are, and we know that their future professional successes depend on them being able to integrate these lessons.

## TEAM BUILDING IN BUSINESS

Even if a person doesn't have previous athletic training, any discipline can hone the same skills that invariably prove useful in building one's family, one's business, one's team. These skills include loyalty, being a team player, and accountability. Another major component of any training is leadership, which we will discuss in depth in the next chapter.

**LOYALTY.** We all know what loyalty means, but we rarely think about how it cements our relationships. Whether personal or professional, loyalty between two people strengthens their bond. It helps you to be united, and whether you are business partners or life partners, you have to be united, confident, and loyal to yourself and to each other. You also have to be loyal to the brand that you're trying to promote and the reputation you're building. It must be the focus of your decision-making.

**BEING A TEAM PLAYER.** There is such value in belonging to something other than yourself, something bigger than yourself. The girls on my golf team and I would've helped each other in any way possible. We were there for each other. We would do whatever we needed to for one another, whether it was on the golf course or off. Being a team player means you are willing to do whatever it takes to be successful. When something needs to be done, you just do it. You want everybody to be successful, not just yourself. For example, I consider the people who work with us at Henderson Properties to work *with* us, not *for* us. When you're a team player, you want the good of the whole group, and you're willing to help motivate each other to succeed. You're not separate, you're united.

**ACCOUNTABILITY.** In sports, in business, and in personal life, you are accountable. You are held accountable whether you succeed or fail. You are held accountable whether your *team* succeeds or fails. One of the problems with today's generation is too many parents and kids want to pass the blame. I think it's important that we take ownership whether good or bad for our actions and we are held accountable to each other. We might as well make it right while we have a chance. If Henderson Properties fails, that's on Phil and me. If Henderson Properties succeeds, that's also on Phil and me. Unfortunately, it's a lot more difficult to accept defeat than it is success.

Because of our reverence for intentional team building, Phil and I understand the importance of waiting for the right people to come our way. The people who are on your team must be loyal, supportive, and motivated. The biggest hurt that I've had in the business is hiring people who have turned out to be different from who I thought they were. It has affected our trust in people, for sure. If you have ever managed people, you know what I am talking about. People can be whoever they want to be on a resume. If you aren't invested or committed to a role—whether that is your marriage, your employment, your education—then it is easy to leave. We have made a conscious effort over the last five years to avoid hiring somebody just because he or she looks good on paper simply because we need to fill a vacancy.

We also apply this same principle on a personal level by working hard on our marriage and on bringing up our family. There are three things I know for sure: the way I want to raise my children, my politics, and my faith. Phil and I try to spend as much time with our kids as we can. They are our top priority, so why wouldn't we? I hope to empower my children and other young people that you don't just find yourself in a circle of peers; you seek them out strategically. Make sure they are building you up, and not tearing you down. It is so important to consciously choose your team—your friends, your partner, your coaches, your co-workers. The first mentor your kids might have is a coach. Think about the life-long effects on that experience. Whether in marriage, family, business, or sports, surround yourself with people who will help you succeed and will encourage you to be the best version of yourself.

## ON TEAM BUILDING

*by Phil Henderson*

I started playing youth-league football at age ten. I was normally one of the best players on the team and sometimes the star of the team. That continued all the way through my senior year in high school. After high school, however, I was not highly recruited and was not offered a scholarship at Appalachian State University. I decided to attend ASU anyway, but I didn't play the fall semester of my first year. After sitting out a season, I decided to try to walk on to the team in the spring of my freshman year.

As a walk-on, no one knew who I was or what kind of success I had had in my high school football career. I was given worn-out equipment to use and treated like a "tackling dummy" in practices. No one gave me any respect, and many of the upperclassmen made fun of me because I didn't have a scholarship. I had to scrape, claw, and fight my way onto the team. By the end of the spring training camp, however, I had made the team. The next season I dressed for all the home games and ended up being a starter on the Junior Varsity team, working my way up to third string on the depth chart at one of our wide-receiver positions on Varsity.

Playing team sports throughout my youth and early adulthood has had a lasting impact on my life. Participating in team sports—football in particular—has made me realize the importance of a team working together. In football, every player has a job to do on every play. If everyone does his job correctly, then the play will be a success. If you're on offense, then that means the team will gain a lot of yards on the play. If you are on defense, it means you'll shut the other team's offense down on that play.

It's similar at Henderson Properties. Our company is structured in smaller teams that provide services to other divisions. For example, our accounting department provides accounting services to both our rental property management division and our association management division. Both divisions depend on the accounting depart-ment to do their jobs correctly and to provide reports in a timely manner to our clients. Consequently, the accounting department depends on those same two divisions to provide them information so that they can do their job effectively. If these departments don't work well together then our service is subpar and, ultimately, our clients suffer.

The team player I became at ASU was the foundation for my leadership training. Team sports helped me hone a positive attitude. In sports, you must believe you can win before you will win. You must have a positive attitude, or you will never win a game. Whether you think you can or you think you can't, you are right. That is true in sports and in business. Daily at Henderson Properties, I have to maintain a positive attitude and outlook for the good of my staff. If I believe we can succeed, then we will.

My sports experience also prepared me for my business life by offering opportunities to practice and cultivate an attitude of perseverance. In sports you must overcome many obstacles such as injuries, bad calls by the referee, or inclement weather. Despite these odds, you must keep working hard to win the game. In my football career, I faced many of these obstacles and learned to overcome them and keep trying my best to win.

The experience with ASU football was similar to when Shelly and I started Henderson Properties. No one knew who we were. No one gave us any respect or credibility. We had to fight, scratch, and claw for everything we got. We had to start from scratch to build the business, just like I did when I walked onto the football team at ASU. These lessons of teamwork and perseverance through football have served me well over the years at Henderson Properties.

## CHAPTER 4

------------------------------

# THE ENTREPRENEURIAL MYTH AND THE REALITIES OF LEADERSHIP

*Leadership is a choice, not a position.*

**—STEPHEN COVEY**

ome years ago, I watched an interview with Oprah Winfrey where she was asked if she felt sorry for the people on airplanes who rode business class while she was enjoying first class or riding in her private jet. She responded that she didn't feel sorry for the other travelers at all, because she knew she had worked hard and earned the right to choose her mode of travel. Though that answer seemed somewhat harsh when I initially heard it, her answer has stuck with me. Before the birth of Henderson Properties, I had given little thought to the entrepreneurial myth. Like most people, I thought that entrepreneurs lived an easy life. They had it all, right? They were their own bosses;

they could vacation when they wanted; they could come and go as they pleased. Money didn't seem like it was a problem. Oh, it must be nice.

*I thought that entrepreneurs lived an easy life. They had it all, right? They were their own bosses; they could vacation when they wanted; they could come and go as they pleased. Money didn't seem like it was a problem. Oh, it must be nice.*

After becoming an entrepreneur, however, I realized that most people only tend to see the happy, shiny side of success. This is the entrepreneurial myth. Sure, some people's success may come easily, but this is rare and there are usually decades of hard work and sacrifice between the birth and the triumph of a business. When you are a business owner, people rarely see what goes on behind the scenes. Entrepreneurs worry about everything. They worry about payroll. They worry about bills. They worry about taxes. They worry about potential theft or burglary. They worry about hiring the right people. There are so many factors of concern for an entrepreneur. It's important to address these misconceptions about the entrepreneur and show what goes on behind the scenes. It would be a disservice not to look more closely at this myth, so that employees and future business owners can learn how believing the falsehood could harm a business's viability before it has even begun.

My decades spent building Henderson Properties from a company of two to now employing sixty staff members, have taught me that people may appear to be successful on the outside, but on the inside, they may be consumed with worrisome thoughts about meeting their next goal and making sure every decision they make is going to enable everybody to get a paycheck. For example, despite the fact that we have been in business for many years, we lost a really big account recently, and privately we went into temporary panic mode. Phil and I decided we could only spend money on necessities. I spent $50 a week on groceries for the next several weeks. I became a (thrifty) master chef by using what we already had on hand to create simple one-pot meals. Maybe that was overkill but saving even a few dollars made us feel calmer in time of a crisis. To an entrepreneur every dollar counts! If you are going to build your own business, it's on you … and I hope you like canned soup! It is true that challenges build character and humility. You cannot be an effective business leader until you acknowledge this myth and understand how and why it differentiates you from your employees.

I recently took a group of Henderson Properties employees to lunch. One of them repeatedly called me "Mrs. Henderson," and I finally told her that I preferred to be called by my first name at work. As I made this request, I realized that I want to think of myself as "one of them"—but my employees don't view me that way. I'm the Entrepreneur, the Boss. I'm different, whether I want to be or not. It's important to understand before becoming "the Boss" that you will be *different* from your staff. You will have to be strong and mature enough to handle their projections, their worries, their frustrations— and when they honestly speak their expectations. When somebody doesn't show up for work or calls in sick, or when you lose several accounts in one month, everything must be reshuffled. That falls to you. An entrepreneur must make the right choices to keep everyone employed. Every decision you make will affect other people and their families. This is a difficult part of being an entrepreneur, and thus, it's important to be prepared for it. You are not a member of the group;

you are the leader of the team, which we will discuss fully in the next section of this chapter.

---

For those readers who are not building their own business, but are looking to further their professional development, this is still an important myth to dispel. If Henderson Properties doesn't succeed, our employees will move on and find other jobs; there are no ties that bind them to us. There's nothing that will hold them accountable to Phil and me. They can walk away with nothing invested, nothing gained, nothing lost. We, on the other hand, will bear that burden and it will affect our finances and livelihood for much longer. Understanding the risks involved makes you more appreciative of your job and its creators. Your employer is taking a risk for you every day. That employer may have done without, maybe for decades, because the business and its success mean that much to him or her. When you fully understand the blood, sweat, and tears of entrepreneurs, there is often more respect for them. This can benefit you professionally when you understand and appreciate all that your employer has done to create the company you work for. As we will discuss in chapter 6, your attitude has a direct correlation to your professional development and potential leadership opportunities. Don't underestimate how a small basic understanding of your employer's service to the company can create a big change in your own professional development.

---

After all these years, Phil and I are still learning and striving to do better and be better. The challenges and struggles are real. The risk and reward are great. Not everyone thinks like an entrepreneur. Not everyone wants to be an entrepreneur. That is okay.

Entrepreneurs play by their own rules. You have a will to create a better life for yourself and those with whom you come in contact. Entrepreneurs don't necessarily want to play by everyone else's rules. If they did, they would be employees instead of bosses. Employees have a guarantee; entrepreneurs have a risk. Employees have jobs that provide benefits and security; entrepreneurs must thrive on uncertainty. Some employees don't like to take blame or constructive criticism; entrepreneurs, however, are culpable even if they aren't directly involved. If you are considering making the move from employee to entrepreneur, you must be realistic about these differences. The entrepreneurs are the ones taking the risk. Therefore, if they succeed, they are entitled to that success; and if they fail, that is their failure. Perhaps that is why Oprah Winfrey's comments at the beginning of this chapter resonated so strongly with me. At some point, as an entrepreneur, you should get to reap the benefits of your work. After years of risks and worries, you should be allowed to enjoy some of the rewards.

There isn't a magic formula for success. Our growth has been steady, though at times a little weathered and weary. There have been days when I have felt somewhat burdened by my role. During those times, I looked at the world with so much expectation that I ended up feeling disappointed. With time, though, I began to notice these expectations and reel them back in. For every disappointment I've felt, there have been just as many opportunities for gratitude. Entrepreneurs wait in the wings, always looking for the next chance to make their mark and create a better way of life, whether by creating jobs, stimulating the economy, leading others to do their best, or by writing a book. I love that my business has created a platform that allows me to inspire and encourage others. I love the good people we have met along the way, the long-term clients, the respectful tenants, the employees who have stuck it out alongside us. These are the rewards that make up for the risks of entrepreneurship. They are not always tangible rewards, but they are profound.

## DID YOU KNOW? AN ENTREPRENEUR'S REALITY:

- There's never a good time to start a business, so just do it!

- The struggle doesn't end, it just evolves.

- Small business owners often, at various times, don't get a paycheck.

- Entrepreneurs often can't take a vacation.

- Perfect work/life balance is impossible.

Not everyone is going to like or agree with you. It is a chance to create something from nothing

## LEADERSHIP

Knowing the realities of entrepreneurship and taking the risk in spite of those is what initiates one's leadership training. When you knowingly throw yourself into entrepreneurship, you have no choice but to become a leader. If you don't force yourself to lead by example, then the outcome is failure, and nobody likes to fail. In business, like in sports, when your team wins, it's a much better day than when it loses. In fact, sports training, and other disciplined endeavors like it, provide valuable leadership training. Making sure that you are involved in many team-building, disciplined activi-

> *When you knowingly throw yourself into entrepreneurship, you have no choice but to become a leader.*

ties is a great way for young people and people taking breaks from the job market to continue to foster their own leadership skills. I'm not sure that I was the best leader in college, but I was developing these skills during my golf training, and leadership roles in my sorority, just as Phil was enriching his own leadership qualities while playing high school and college football. These groups have made us the leaders we are today, and we're proud and grateful to have been surrounded by various personal and professional connections who have enriched our leadership styles.

Leadership qualities evolve over time, but sometimes you're forced to become the leader out of necessity. When Phil and I decided to start Henderson Properties, it wasn't to become leaders. As we have grown, however, we've been put into that position, and we now have sixty people who depend on our guidance. Being the leaders and having our name on the building means that with every success we enjoy, there's always the possibility of failure that we would also have to endure.

There are many leadership qualities that Phil and I both share, which creates a solid foundation for our company. We are both schedule-driven, task-oriented people. The glass is always half full; the snow is never too deep to drive in. Where there's a will, there's a way. One thing that Phil has taught me about being a leader, is that if you can't find a way, then *make* the way. Don't settle for "no." Do whatever it takes to get the job done. Despite these similarities in our work ethics, Phil and I are different in our leadership styles. Phil is the planner, the goal-setter. I am more of the visionary, the worker, the lead-by-example type. There are many ways to lead. It is important to know your own strengths and weaknesses, so you can fully understand your leadership style. Once you have this self-awareness, you know exactly what you can offer a company. The goal is to lead where you are; whether at the top, the middle, or the bottom.

Since leadership skills evolve over time, your style is not static. My definition of leadership is much different now than when I was twenty-two. As a young adult, you might want to be a leader, but you're not sure enough of yourself at that point and you don't want to stick out of the crowd and draw attention to yourself. You're still trying to hide behind that mask of who you want to be, not necessarily who you *are*. As an adult, however, I want to stick out in a crowd; I want to be noticed; I want to be the best. With maturation, I've also become more realistic, but my expectations are a lot higher than they used to be. I think that being a leader means you set the bar high for yourself and for the people around you. At times this is a risk that may cause some disappointment because people aren't always going to meet your expectations. I am totally guilty of this and am constantly working on it. When I have it figured out I will let you know.

*As an adult, however, I want to stick out in a crowd; I want to be noticed; I want to be the best. With maturation, I've also become more realistic, but my expectations are a lot higher than they used to be.*

In many ways, leadership is different for men and women. Women are oftentimes skilled at multitasking and being more flexible. I sometimes remind Phil that he has a wife and an assistant to help him. I've got no one. I don't have an assistant, so I have to create my own structure. Professionals who have families or other responsibilities with little to no support will understand that sometimes you can't stay focused on one task. It's impossible. If you're at home with children who need something while you're working on a business project, you don't have the luxury of staying on task. That's the reality. Rather than let this be frustrating, we can view it as a helpful exercise in leadership training. It is frustrating to be doing many things at once, but the person who can do that often and well might be more hirable than someone who cannot.

I'd like to take a moment here to address those readers who may have taken a professional hiatus to raise children or be caretakers. This is not a liability. This is another myth that must be dispelled. *Being a parent or a caretaker does not preclude you from being a successful professional.* Having been an employee, a business owner, and a mother, I can say without hesitation, that being a parent is a professional asset and has the capacity to differentiate you from others. We will talk more about the challenges of parenting and professionalism in the next chapter, but it is important to note here that being a parent or caretaker does foster an exceptional skill set that can benefit an employer. I challenge you to include this in a resume. What a great conversation starter that would set you apart from the rest.

Becoming a parent had a profound effect on my leadership skills. Once my sons were born, it became important to foster their growth in the *right* ways. Sure, I would have loved for them to be straight "A" students, but my time spent as an entrepreneur confirmed that there

> *If you're at home with children who need something while you're working on a business project, you don't have the luxury of staying on task. That's the reality. Rather than let this be frustrating, we can view it as a helpful exercise in leadership training.*

were other qualities as important as their educational success. It was just as important to me that my sons excelled at sports, as it was important that they be part of a team and be gracious enough to thank the coaches after practice. My goal was that they become well rounded. Blake and Grant are both leaders in their own ways. With my children, I tried to pick out their strengths and weaknesses and encourage their leadership skills based on their individual skill sets. Those are still evolving—and I wouldn't have it any other way.

*Becoming a parent had a profound effect on my leadership skills. Once my sons were born, it became important to foster their growth in the right ways.*

With my decades as an entrepreneur and my new understanding of leadership skills, I recently have felt called to lead in other areas of my life. I wanted to increase my involvement in my church. After several months of trying to talk myself out of it, I took the plunge. I became a volunteer to facilitate a life group, formed by me thanks to other friends who were searching for the same kind of spiritual fulfillments, which provides leadership and faith-building skills to families in our congregation and community. As of this writing, I am proud to say my life group consists of five families who have met biweekly on a regular basis

*Since this has become such an enriching opportunity for me and for our staff, I will offer specific advice from my leadership training methods in chapter 9. In these classes, I encourage staff to be leaders in their lives.*

since the spring of 2015. I felt so empowered by helping people, and myself, become better that I wanted to bring something similar to our company. Since this has become such an enriching opportunity for me and for our staff, I will offer specific advice from my leadership training methods in chapter 9. In these classes, I encourage staff to be leaders in their lives. It doesn't have to all be in the business world. You can be a leader on your sports team. You can be a leader in the classroom or at church. Know yourself well and be brave enough to offer your gifts to your family, your employer, your staff, or your community to lead from within.

Make no mistake, being a leader is not always the same as being in charge. Sometimes the leader has to evolve, and sometimes that means stepping back and letting someone else lead. In the beginning, it was Phil and I working together, side by side, day in and day out. About ten years into the business, I found myself needing to take a step back, because I felt like there only needed to be one Henderson in charge. I decided that my leadership capabilities would be better used elsewhere. It was a bold step that I made, but it was the right choice at the time for the company and for my family.

Another aspect of leadership is learning to manage your own guilt. When you're a leader and so many people depend on you— clients, customers, employees—you may feel guilty when you go on vacation, *if* you get to take vacation at all. This is another myth of entrepreneurship. It seems like a business owner can vacation anytime he or she wants; the reality, however, is that Phil and I didn't take a weeklong vacation for the first twelve years of owning the company. In the summer of 2016, we decided we were going to take nine days off and take our family to Europe. On the way to the airport, we received a call that our whole e-mail server system had crashed. At that time, we had five satellite offices, more than 800 rental properties to manage, and better than 140 homeowner-association communities. No one could be reached, and we couldn't send an e-mail alerting people that we were experiencing trouble. We didn't know what to do. Do we turn the car around or do we keep going? A few years into the business, we would have canceled our trip. But as seasoned veterans, we knew the company was sound enough to carry on, so we decided to keep going. We had faith in the leaders of our team, and we were confident in the skills they had been building during their time with Henderson Properties.

> *As seasoned veterans, we knew the company was sound enough to carry on, so we decided to keep going. We had faith in the leaders of our team.*

Not all people are called to lead at the top or in front. Others need to follow or to be the "cheerleaders." The important part of leadership is not receiving all the glory, it's differentiating yourself from the majority of people. It's holding yourself and those around you to higher standards. A leader is someone who recognizes his or her mistakes and admits them, but then takes the even more challenging step of incorporating those mistakes and improving from them. Everybody can be a leader in some way—if he or she wants to. The only questions are where do you want to make a difference, and where do you want to make your mark in this world? We all have a calling. It is up to us to find it. Start small. It begins with a desire and purpose. Have you found yours?

As the leader of your business, you must make time to enjoy what you have created. I am satisfied with the hard work I've put in since the beginning, and I want to continue to be successful. I've got no problem saying I'm proud of Henderson Properties. I'm grateful for our employees. I love the people I work with. I'm so proud of how far we've come and where we are going. Everything we have gone through professionally has gotten us where we are today. Whatever decisions were made—right or wrong—we survived, and I'm so proud of that.

## ON LEADERSHIP

### by Phil Henderson

Throughout my life, I've always been in leadership positions, though not always by my own choice. As a teenager and young adult, I was put in leadership positions mainly because of my athletic ability. I don't think I really exhibited any leadership abilities; it just happened since I was one of the better players on the team. Looking back on those years, I don't think I was a very good leader as I didn't always set a good example. In my college and early adult years, I didn't really focus on leadership and was mainly focused on myself. This all changed when I became a parent and a business owner.

Leadership means you have to focus on the people you are leading. In parenting, I've had to focus on setting a good example for my boys. That comes with the language I use, the work ethic I show, and the daily habits I keep. Before I make any decision, I think *what would Blake and Grant think about me doing this?* As a parent, especially a parent of boys, the children will follow the actions of their father. That is a lot of pressure, but it holds me accountable, and it has enriched my leadership abilities.

In business, my leadership style has evolved over the years. Early in our business life, I had never managed people. Unfortunately, I didn't hire a lot of the right people, so I was leading a staff that performed poorly. Those two factors made it hard for me to trust that our employees were doing things correctly and efficiently. This led me to micromanage. With experience, my leadership style—and hiring practices—have changed, and I am now a more trusting, confident leader. I try to be an encourager, a coach, and more of a "partner" with the employees who report directly to me.

One thing that all leaders must do is continue to improve their leadership skills. The best way to do this is by reading books, attending seminars, or finding business groups that have effective leaders willing to pass on what they've learned. Shelly has started a blog that offers valuable information on leadership and would be helpful to many employers and employees alike. Leaders aren't born overnight. They are made over the course of a person's life, by integrating personal successes and failures. Be honest with yourself about your leadership style. Take all opportunities to cultivate it and share it in positive ways at work and at home.

# CHAPTER 5

------------------------------

# A SEAT AT THE TABLE

*At a round table there's no dispute of place.*

**—PROVERB**

My family of four has been sitting at the same round table for sixteen years. It's heavy and sturdy, and it's the one piece of furniture I don't think I could ever part with. It's where the four of us have gathered to eat, play games, and have many family meetings and talks. The size is perfect. The circular shape means there's no head. We've moved two separate times with that table, and each time we place it in a new kitchen, we claim our same spots. When my sons return home from college, they immediately resume their seats as if they'd never left. I suppose returning to the same space becomes habitual and in some small way brings us comfort and security.

In that way, the conference table at work is no different than our table at home. We all gravitate to the seat we filled before; we are a dynamic blend of personalities and backgrounds all working for a common goal. Like family, we sometimes argue or disagree, but we're all in it together. When balancing a family, a business, and a myriad of responsibilities, you become skilled at realizing when things start shifting at your table. When that happens, your responsibilities—and your literal and figurative seat at the table—oftentimes must change.

As I have mentioned, on August 14, 2002, my son Blake, who was seven at the time, was diagnosed with type 1 diabetes, an auto-immune disease where the pancreas stops producing insulin; it's not caused by diet or eating too much sugar. He was diagnosed at a routine doctor's appointment, one week before school started. We were shocked and devastated. It was one of the many parenting moments when I had to become the calm and composed leader of the family so as not to induce worry in my son. Our whole world changed. Gone were the quick trips to the grocery store; now my grocery-store trips were three-hour journeys reading labels and counting carbohydrates. Now we had a staff at the endocrinologist's office and appointments every quarter. I learned how to give insulin shots, fill a syringe, and calculate carbs into an insulin-to-carbohydrate ratio based on what foods he was eating at each meal. Gone were the peaceful nights of sleep. Now there were finger pricks every two to three hours round the clock to check his blood sugar and treat him accordingly. The public school wasn't as equipped back then, and because he was so young I was asked to come in daily and help Blake administer

*My son needed me. He needed me at home and the school needed me readily available. So, I gave up my seat at the work table and resumed my seat at the family table.*

his insulin before lunch and check his blood-sugar levels. My seat at the conference table became vacant, because my attention was diverted. My son needed me. He needed me at home and the school needed me readily available. So, I gave up my seat at the work table and resumed my seat at the family table.

If I had been in business by myself, I'm not sure the business would've survived, because I had to step away for several months until we got ourselves together and my son could function at school. If your blood sugar gets too high, you throw up; if you throw up at school, they send you home; if you miss too many days of school, you don't pass the grade. Now coming down with even the flu was risky. This was my dilemma. What is more important? Having a business so I can support my family or keeping my child's health and educational future on track? It was an impossible scenario. It never gets easier, and I feel it's important that people know this going in to entrepreneurship. Balancing work life and home life is never a simple thing. The benefit of being an entrepreneur, however, is that those who are brave enough can step away when they are needed elsewhere. One reason it's so important to hire the right people is so that you have a supportive, adept team around your table, whether you're there or not. Being an entrepreneur gives you options, especially if you have leadership and/or a supportive husband as your business partner, like I have had. I was so grateful that I was able to step away and give my son's health the attention it deserved. But eventually finding my way back again. The flexibility is a huge benefit.

When life happens, as it always does, we must recognize when to get up and change seats. Phil often says to our staff that he's

> *When life happens, as it always does, we must recognize when to get up and change seats.*

glad to have them on the bus, but he wants to be certain everyone is in the right seat on the bus. I have found this to be true in both professional and personal realms. In 2011, the real estate market was struggling. Businesses were laying off workers and many were closing their doors permanently. We lost accounts. We lost employees. We lost business. We were stressed; our employees were stressed. Unfortunately, at that time, we had some staff members who had negative attitudes, and considering the economic downturn, it seemed everyone was on edge. I found myself wanting to step away from Henderson Properties. I questioned myself, our business direction, and some of the people we had on staff. I was hugely affected by other's attitudes and took it too personally. At this time, I felt strongly that two Hendersons weren't needed at the table. I could see the stress that work was putting on our family. The future was not looking bright for our business. I decided rather than offer my children two stressed parents, I would yet again step aside from Henderson Properties and let Phil take the lead seat to ensure there was some sort of peace at home. My oldest son was starting high school at the time, and my younger son was in middle school. It seemed every which way we turned, there was a hurdle to overcome, both personally and professionally. Those of you who have kids in the midst of middle and high school would agree. We took it day to day. The only viable option for me was to give up my seat at the work table and focus on what was happening around my family table. It truly was a season of life that was face paced with the boys' sports, extracurricular activities, and trying to balance the expectations and challenges of the business during that recession period. By the grace of God we all survived!

Was it easy to relinquish my seat at the conference table? No. I missed being at the helm of Henderson Properties, and I felt guilty, but I also felt like my time was needed elsewhere at least for the time being. I just needed to take a break, and if I didn't, I wasn't sure what the outcome would be. I wasn't sure if we would sell the business. I wasn't sure if our marriage would sustain the stress. I wasn't sure if my children would continue to thrive. I knew at that particular time I needed to take a step back and find other ways to lead. We ultimately survived this period, and our business experienced continued growth through the next few years, but I never forgot how difficult it was to give up my seat at the table. Relinquishing your seat is scary and humbling. I took a step back knowing that if I wasn't as involved, I might not get a say in the direction the company was headed. Although I have never regretted that it was the right decision at the time, I did learn how important it was to listen to your gut when it comes to balancing your work and home lives. If you have the opportunity to step away when you need to I recommend it. If you don't you need to seek support in other ways; family, business support groups etc ...

For the next several months, I resumed my job as head of the household, and Phil went back to working twelve to fourteen-hour days. The negative staff members eventually left or were fired, and we experienced our greatest turnover ever. The tumultuous trend continued for some time, and it became evident I needed to try to convert the chaos of work/life balance into peace, both at home and the office. Phil's expectations at home and the office were ramped up. My stress level escalated. My sons were going through puberty. To add more chaos to an already hectic time, we moved to a larger home centrally located to our life. Phil said if I found a good deal we could move. It took patience, but after eighteen months I found a deal in the neighborhood we'd been dreaming of for years. Through it all, I found myself trying to survive day-by-day, hoping Phil wouldn't come home at the end of a long day with more news of losing accounts and/or staff.

During the economic downturn that began in 2008, we had to freeze pay increases, though we never had to lay anyone off or cut anyone's hours. After the crisis, however, we were able to go back and honor those raises. Through all our mistakes, challenges, and perseverance, we came through, knowing that we had learned a valuable lesson about hiring positive employees to fill the seats. It wasn't as important who filled what seat as it was that we have a common attitude of positivity and respect. *Coachable and trainable* became our new yardsticks when hiring. We knew we couldn't build a team without people. Now we knew we couldn't build a business without the *right* people. From that day forth, our mission has been to get the right people in the right seats, and that goes for Phil and me too.

During this time of me shuffling from one seat to another to meet the needs of the company, Phil has remained in one seat, as president of the company. Always has been, always will be. You can't have two cooks in the kitchen, right? My being flexible and able to do many jobs is an invaluable asset. As an entrepreneur or as any kind of businessperson, you must know when your role has to shift, whether it's a positive or negative one. Sometimes it's obvious when your role must change. For example, when I was working in accounts payable, we started to have sustained growth, and I recognized that I was getting in over my head; we needed to hire an accounting manager. So, we did just that. There was no room for pride or ego. I had to recognize it was time to give my seat to someone more qualified.

> There was no room for pride or ego. I had to recognize it was time to give my seat to someone more qualified.

Though this shuffling around may sound frustrating to some, I viewed the transitions in a positive way, since I was adding to my skill set. Now I am more experienced in the daily functioning of the company than anyone else, and I take pride in that, because it's not easy to remain so pliable. Multi-tasking? Wearing many hats? Doing many jobs? I did that each and every day at home and at the office. As I discussed in the previous chapter, it is my hope that mothers and fathers can see how much their home life with their children is preparing them to be better leaders. For many parents, it seems like one life stops when you become a parent, and another life starts; but it's all one beautiful, chaotic life. Having children enriches life and, surprisingly enough, requires you to strengthen the same skills needed at work. This is not the message stay-at-home parents often hear in our culture. Parents who go to work often feel guilty, while some parents stay at home and often feel guilty. Many parents are forced to choose all or nothing. They spend all their time at work or they spend all their time at home. Being an entrepreneur means you get to decide the ratio. That's an incredible reward. I don't go to the office every day, and I do feel some guilt about that, but I also feel like I get to enjoy a home life as well as a work life, and that's a reward.

In business, just as in parenting, nobody is going to love your company as much as you do. It's easy to walk away when your name isn't on the building. It's very easy to give your opinion, good, bad, or indifferent, if your name is not on the building. In business and in family, there is a constant struggle of a family within a family. You have many different personalities and you will wonder daily if you can ever measure up to their expectations.

> *In business, just as in parenting, nobody is going to love your company as much as you do. It's easy to walk away when your name isn't on the building.*

Many cognizant business owners understand the connection between home life and work life, and they try to honor it as much as possible. One of the best ways to enrich your own professional experience is to find a work environment where people are willing to fill your seat if your family needs you. Furthermore, if you are a business owner concerned with staff retention, this is the greatest way to keep your employees happy. Use the list below to gauge how flexible your workplace is. Use the answers to open a dialogue with your employer or human resources personnel. These questions are also helpful when interviewing for a new job. Remember that your employer wants to keep you happy. There is nothing wrong with trying to determine how supportive he or she is of a work/life balance.

## HOW SUPPORTIVE IS YOUR BUSINESS OF YOUR WORK/LIFE BALANCE?

- If I have a sick child at home, can I use sick time, or must I use personal leave?

- If there is a problem or emergency at my child's school, how would the business handle my abrupt departure?

- Are other employees cross-trained to be able to complete my tasks if I am unable to be at work?

- How receptive is my employer to hearing my interests in switching seats/job duties if I see a position I feel is right for me?

So much of being a successful entrepreneur is knowing when to claim your seat at the management table and when to relinquish it. It's about hiring the right people to fulfill your lifelong dream as an entrepreneur. What I learned from stepping away from the table is that you cannot do everything on your own. The right people rise to the occasion. You have to make sure that your business is supportive. It is crucial that you fill your seats with positive, hardworking individuals. Take note that I mentioned "positive" first. Find people who are competent, confident, flexible, and willing to shift seats if you can't be there. I reiterate: people who are coachable and trainable. Hire for attitude and aptitude!

During unforeseen circumstances, it is so comforting to be able to step aside and give your attention to the area of your life that is in need. Sometimes that's your family; sometimes that's your own health. Being an entrepreneur allows you to find the right people for the right seats, so that if you must leave your seat temporarily, you can be confident in your team's performance. Stepping away from the table doesn't mean you don't care. It means you care deeply about your family, yourself, and life's other priorities. We are all busy juggling and balancing, and it is empowering to know that at Henderson Properties, we have created a work environment that allows people the opportunity to take care of themselves and their families when they need it most.

---------------------------------------------------------

## HENDERSON PROPERTIES EMPLOYEE SPOTLIGHT:

*I have been with Henderson Properties for over five years. I've served in several positions, including executive assistant, executive coordinator, and marketing coordinator.*

*When I came to Henderson Properties to interview, it felt like home. What keeps me here is the atmosphere. Many of us call this our "work family," because it's team-oriented. We are committed to learning and growing together. We share lessons learned and encourage each other to be our best selves. We help each other in busy times and train in less busy moments.*

*Henderson Properties is also faith and values-centric, and one of the core values is to demonstrate honest and ethical behavior in all business transactions. Because I have a strong faith and desire to conduct business honestly, the matching core values make this a great place to work.*

*The leadership also promotes social responsibility, and models this through charitable giving and participation. Each year, we host a food drive to benefit the local area's less fortunate. The company also launched a paid-day option for staff to volunteer with a local charity.*

*One of my goals as marketing coordinator has been to bridge the gap between marketing messages and operational efficiency. This means to deliver on what we promise in our marketing message. I've enjoyed working through this process and creating communication lines between the division managers, marketing, and sales.*

**KELLY WALLACE**
*Marketing Coordinator*

-------------------------------------------------------------

# CHAPTER 6

----------------------------------

# LIVING THE DREAM

*Opportunity is missed by most people because it is
dressed in overalls and looks like work.*

**— THOMAS EDISON**

I never set out to live the American dream. In fact, it wasn't until
recently that I even recognized my life today represents this
ideal. For Phil and me, the American dream looked different
than it did for my maternal great grandparents who came to
America in the early 1900s. Their dream was probably more about
freedom and liberty. For Phil and me, the dream was about creating
something out of nothing and capitalizing on an opportunity. We
took a hobby and decided we could make a living out of it. The
dream was about two people willing to work hard, all day, every day,
no matter what—whether we were sick or stressed or out of money.

Pursuing the American dream, which had once involved
dangerous sea voyages and acclimating to a new culture, had by the

1980s and '90s became more about achieving financial prosperity. We started Henderson Properties during a time when the images of rich and successful people included the characters on TV shows like *Dynasty* and *Dallas*. Though they certainly had their share of drama and intrigue, few of the characters had storylines about them "starting from scratch." The rich and famous were born rich and famous; they died rich and famous. Where were their blood, sweat, and tears? We didn't have too many cultural icons of people making something from nothing.

*For Phil and me, the American dream looked different than it did for my maternal great grandparents who came to America in the early 1900s. Their dream was probably more about freedom and liberty. For Phil and me, the dream was about creating something out of nothing and capitalizing on an opportunity.*

We didn't see that we were trying to make the American dream a reality for ourselves. We saw an opportunity for our family, and we decided we'd get to work trying to make it happen. During this time, computer technology was taking off, and banks didn't seem to mind that Phil and I wanted to purchase one real estate foreclosure after another. Our heads were buried deep in the logistics of trying to make a go of it, and we had the added distraction of sleepless nights and changing lots of dirty diapers. We didn't know much other than we were in survival mode, and we didn't want to fail.

As I write this, we still have the same purpose. We don't want to fail; we want to succeed and keep growing. At this point, we may seem to others to have it all, but exactly what does it mean to have it all? We may seem to have financial security, but when you own your own business, is one ever completely financially secure? We try to prepare. We save money. We are slow to make financial decisions. But, as we all know, the economy and having it all can come crashing down without notice.

Getting Henderson Properties through the financial crisis of 2008–2012 was an important and enriching time for our company. As I mentioned in the previous chapter, this was one of the most challenging phases for our business and our family. But it also reminded us that the American dream is not just about reaping benefits. It's about persistence, it's about the struggle, and it's about resilience. The financial crisis happened so quickly that

*Getting Henderson Properties through the financial crisis of 2008–2012 was an important and enriching time for our company.*

there wasn't a lot of time to prepare. Not only did it teach us that we must be ready for a crisis, but that we also must build a resilient, determined staff. So, perhaps one of the most valuable aspects of pursuing the American dream is in the struggle, in the humbling knowledge that success can be taken away at any moment.

One cannot persevere during challenging times like these without faith. Faith in the business you've built, faith in your leadership skills, and faith in the quality and abilities of your employees. As I mentioned in the last chapter, we made a conscious effort to be discerning about whom we hired to make sure we weren't hiring people just to fill the seat—as we had sometimes done in the past out of desperation. The only doubt during this time was not knowing how much Phil could sustain. How much could one person take? I knew if he had the right support at home and at the office that he could ride out the storm.

Fortunately, we survived the crisis, but we were not unscathed. It was a devastating time for our family and business. I hope my children don't remember it. Strangely, though, the aspect I think about the most is that we ended up having one of the most productive years of our business during that time. How could this be, since we were short-staffed and our resources were limited? We owe all of it to our staff! They put in so much hard work and positive energy, that I know this was what carried Phil and me and the business through. Hearing stories about others less fortunate made us all grateful that it wasn't the case at Henderson Properties. I think the silver lining in the downturn of the economy was that people were more appreciative of their jobs. They were happier to come to work. There was more of a sense of gratitude. We saw an inspiring rise in camaraderie on staff. All of which showed us that during a crisis, a leadership team must focus on morale. No matter what else is happening within the company, you must first think of your staff. We needed everybody to keep the morale up. We needed the management team to encourage the staff and support Phil. Because of the interconnectedness of our employees, particularly during a crisis, this experience changed our hiring practices forever.

*During a crisis, a leadership team must focus on morale. No matter what else is happening within the company, you must first think of your staff.*

Before the crisis, we often hired the best candidate on *paper*— meaning the one with the most education, experience, and training. This is what many human resources departments do. It makes rational sense, but we'd learned that a crisis is unexpected and irrational. Now, our hiring model is different. We want to hire people who are coachable and trainable. If you have somebody who wants to learn and wants to be a part of the team, that's everything. But if you've got somebody who is in it for themselves, for the paycheck only, they don't care about team building and positive attitudes I would not hire them. Sometimes though the old saying is true "you don't really know someone until you live with them." Employers need to focus their energies on hiring the right people with the right attitudes, just as jobseekers need to be mindful of their trainability and their attitudes.

After the valuable lessons we learned during the financial crisis, we now aim to create an empathetic culture in our business. Our theme has been *People First*, whether that's employees, clients, tenants, or board members in our homeowner-association communities. This is something I discuss at length in my leadership groups at work. I also remind people that it's important to *communicate before you terminate*. This has helped lower our turnover rate. It requires more from both employee and employer. There must be open communication and a conversation. We will discuss this more fully in chapter 8, but *People First* means keeping business human, visceral. It means approaching your work life like you would your home life. For example, when I get upset with Phil, am I supposed to leave him because we had a bad day? No, I would talk to him and give him the opportunity to hear my perspective and give voice to his own. Isn't it easier to talk to your current boss about an unpleasant situation rather than going through the hassle of quitting your job, interviewing for a new one, and then acclimating yourself to a new work environment? We need to create work environments that allow opportunities to communicate and negotiate. Some employers are not willing to hear your grievances, so how can they remedy them? Those are the workplaces you avoid. At home and at work, the grass is not always greener on the other side. You've got to water your lawn and take care of it so that you know its potential before you walk away.

> *At home and at work, the grass is not always greener on the other side. You've got to water your lawn and take care of it so that you know its potential before you walk away.*

At Henderson Properties, we try to create a culture of empowerment. We want people to feel inspired so that if they do choose to leave us, it's for something that better suits their personal and professional goals. Does it always happen that way? No. Life isn't perfect, and people make up their own minds. If an employee has one foot out the door, it's hard to stop him or her from walking away. How does an employer keep that from happening? The key is to start from the top. Management is the key to success. As one person, Phil can only do so much; our hope is that—by creating an environment that helps staff meet their personal and/or professional goals—we can enrich and empower them. If you choose coachable people, then embolden them and give them tools, there shouldn't be any issue that can't be fixed. However, both the employee and employer have to have the same positive mind set and values.

We have sixty people on staff. It's like a large family that spends time together every day. Not everybody is going to get along. Not everybody is going to agree, but that's okay because if we did, it might get a little boring. We also encourage and promote a culture of support and team building. For instance, we have one employee whose nineteen-year-old son is recovering from cancer. Watching the love and support he received from our work family was inspiring. Recently we've had another staff member who is fighting cancer. Staff members donated their personal time off and did all they could to help. This wasn't about the company. It wasn't about profit. It was about connection and putting people first. Witnessing the graciousness within the walls of our offices has given me a sense of pride. We have several people on staff who have celebrated five and ten-year anniversaries with us. We have one special star who has been with us fifteen years, and one who retired and has come back over and over to help with various projects. This is one of our greatest strengths as a company and one of our greatest rewards. Supporting the people who have invested their time and energy in our company is one of my life's greatest pleasures.

-------------------------------------------------------------

As a job seeker, it's important to think about your attitude when you're going into an interview. It's not necessarily about your training or your education. Although those are significant, it's equally important to consider what you are contributing to the team—so employers know, for instance, that if there is some kind of crisis, you will be supportive and appreciative. As we learned in the economic crisis, creating a culture that puts people first might be the factor that ultimately saves the business. Keep this in mind when doing your own job seeking. Use the list below when preparing for a job interview, whether you are the prospective employee or the employer.

## IDEAL TRAITS FOR EMPLOYEES:

- Trainable and coachable
- Desire to be part of a team
- Hardworking

- Persistent

- Skilled communicator

- Rule following

- Accountable

- Appreciative of job opportunity

- Has a positive attitude

- Emotionally intelligent

-----------------------------------------------------------

Sometimes I wonder if the American dream will be a possibility for millennials. There's a reason why universities have a leadership minor these days, and I'm thinking it isn't because it is popular. It's likely more of a necessity. The tycoon shows of the '80s and '90s have been replaced by reality shows that glamorize the rich and famous. The viewer is left wondering *how* these young people became successful. You used to build a business; now you build a brand. I'm worried that this new example of instant gratification and brand building is altering the definition of the American dream, if not obliterating it all together. Hard work seems antiquated, but as Phil and I have learned, there are abundant rewards for pursuing something you love and working hard for it. There is pride in that, and perhaps that is the greatest reward of pursuing the American dream. I hope that we can instill these values in today's youth. I hope that we can remind them that hard work has a greater payoff than just a financial one. I hope the next generation will continue to create workplace cultures that are empowering for all and will learn from the previous generation. My generation lived the first 30 years of their lives without technology and social media. It can be done. Putting people first, communicating, and working together is what cultivates success.

---

## REWARDS OF PURSUING THE AMERICAN DREAM

- Flexibility when needing to step away (see chapter 5).

- Building faith in yourself and the staff.

- Fostering a workplace culture that supports people and empowers them.

- Pride in creating something from nothing.

- Learning your own personal strengths and weaknesses.

- Seeing the resilience and tenacity of staff.

- Gaining opportunities to provide services and support to community.

- Watching staff enrich and empower their families and communities.

- Opportunities to stay humble.

- Strengthening people skills and communication skills.

- Determining your work/life ratio (see chapter 5).

- The validation from having long-term staff who *choose* to stay with the company.

- The satisfaction that comes with a day of hard work.

---

We are all born to win. Everyone wants success in life, though each person would define that differently. Winning keeps one motivated. Phil and I are no exception. For us, the American dream was not about becoming rich and famous. It was about finding what we truly wanted to do and figuring how to make a life together doing that. We're realistic about the risks and stress and worries, and we don't expect any grand rewards. If Phil and I could capitalize on the

American dream, anybody can. We didn't *acquire* our business. We didn't get a loan. We didn't have family money. We *built* this business from scratch. We worked hard for it. If you don't want to work, you're not going to find the opportunities. Open your eyes, turn up the corners of your mouth, and roll up your sleeves; your American dream is waiting.

## ON THE AMERICAN DREAM

### by Phil Henderson

The financial crisis hit the South in early 2008. Suddenly no one wanted to buy houses for fear of devaluation. Those who did want to buy found it difficult to purchase as lenders adopted stricter credit and income qualifications. Housing values were declining, whereas for the past seventy years, they had been increasing. This was uncharted territory for everyone in the real estate business.

We didn't panic—we prayed a lot, but we didn't panic. Shelly and I talked a lot about what to do with this ever-changing landscape in the real estate sales and management world. I spoke with our management team at length about the situation our industry was in, and we collaborated on what to do. I informed everyone that even though many other real estate firms were laying off employees or filing for bankruptcy, we had no intentions of doing either. However, I had to make the tough decision to reduce the amount of eligible salary increases for one year during 2009. We cut back on lots of other areas within our business to try to keep our overhead as low as possible. This "watch every penny of expense" mentality has stayed with me ever since.

Though the number of sales transactions that our realtors were involved in decreased, we started to notice an increase in our new property-management clients. Home owners who needed to sell their homes were having difficulty, so many came to us to rent their properties for them. Many other homeowners who had purchased new homes didn't want to sell their existing ones, since the prices were much lower now. Many of those homeowners also came to us to utilize our property-management services. So, while our sales division was hurting, our property-management division began to explode. This is another lesson I learned from that crisis: It's a good idea to diversify your business, so when one area of the economy is bad, you can benefit in other areas of your business.

During the financial crisis, there was much worry and stress on our staff. Many were concerned that we would have to lay off employees, since many other businesses were doing just that. Many fretted that we may have to close our business. During that time, I became more of a "cheerleader" in our monthly staff meetings and with our management team. It was important for me to frequently reassure our team that everything was okay, and we were doing fine, even though all the news about the economy and particularly the real estate industry was negative.

During this time of struggle, our staff seemed to grow closer. I think this was due to us communicating to the entire staff about what was going on and what our plans were to deal with it. I believe it gave everyone the sense that we were in this thing together. The management team also became more aware of the emotions of our team. We had to be tuned into the fears of our staff so that we could address them. This led us to be a staff-centric workplace, which our employees appreciated and benefited from.

I believe the American dream of owning your own business and making it successful is more possible now than ever before. Even though previous government administrations were not pro-business, we now, in 2018, have an administration in Washington, DC, that is trying hard to remove many of the burdensome regulations for small businesses and reduce the arduous tax burden put on small-business owners. This, coupled with advancements in technology and the current economic growth, makes the country wide open for anyone who wants to be an entrepreneur and chase financial freedom.

My advice to the millennials who have interests in entrepreneurship is that you better get ready to work. I'm living proof that you don't have to be brilliant to be a successful entrepreneur. However, I attribute my success to my commitment to completing tasks and maintaining a "whatever it takes" attitude. Success as an entrepreneur is preceded by lots of hard work and having a commitment to the task. You can't give up. I say this specifically to the millennial generation because what I see in young adults today is somewhat of an "entitlement" mentality. Many grew up getting the "participation trophy" in their youth sports leagues, and they've, therefore, become accustomed to getting something regardless of how hard they worked or whether they won or lost. That's not the way it works in business. In business, there are winners and losers, and quite frankly the winners are the ones who plan the best and work the hardest.

# CHAPTER 7

------------------------------

# ACCEPTING MY JOURNEY

*All our dreams can come true, if we have the courage to pursue them.*

**— WALT DISNEY**

I recently attended two summer weddings and found myself paying close attention to the couples' vows. They were all filled with optimism, hope, and visions of bright futures. It struck me during these weddings how similar marriage vows are to shared goal setting. A couple makes a plan, then they believe in it, they commit to it, they maintain faith in it. I thought of all the times Phil and I have chosen to hold one another close in support during tough times and remain committed and bold in our pursuit of shared happiness. For our honeymoon, Phil and I enjoyed a blissful week at a Sandals resort in Jamaica. As newlyweds, the future was boundless, and I reveled in the optimism Phil and I shared. Looking back, I see how much of our path was unknown. Was it the naiveté of young love that kept me hopeful—or was it something greater?

One specific evening during our honeymoon, we relaxed in a hammock with a bottle of champagne and the beautiful Caribbean Sea stretching before us. As we chatted about what our daily life might look like back at home as newlyweds, we discussed our professional goals. We talked about the flexibility we wanted and the risks that went along with that level of professional freedom. By the end of the night (and the bottle of champagne) we decided we wanted, at some point, to be entrepreneurs. Later in our marriage, Phil told me that night on the beach was the first time he uttered aloud that he wanted to own his own business, and he felt like declaring it had held him accountable. I'm not sure if it was goal setting in action or the bottle of champagne, but some magic seemed to surround us that night, and the seed of Henderson Properties was planted. Cheers to champagne! We left Jamaica and returned home to our careers—my teaching job and Phil's sales job.

*Later in our marriage, Phil told me that night on the beach was the first time he uttered aloud that he wanted to own his own business, and he felt like declaring it had held him accountable.*

We continued to talk about the future, but we were happy and content for the moment. We knew that when the time was right to take the risks we discussed on our honeymoon, we would know. This certainty and peace was the start of a shared faith that we have continued to cultivate. It wasn't a question of *if* or *how*. It became more of a question of *what* and *when*. We had faith in the goal we set, and we had faith that we could accomplish that goal together.

Both Phil and I came into our marriage with a strong faith in God. We came from different Christian denominations—Phil was

Baptist, and I was Catholic. He was willing to convert, but we felt more led to the Baptist sermons, so for the first fifteen years of our marriage, we attended a Baptist church. My faith while attending this church grew. I remember one sermon entitled "The Storms of Your Life." I recall wondering what my storms would be. I used the teachings and notes of that sermon some six months later when Blake was diagnosed with diabetes. I have returned to these teachings over and over in my home and work life. The storms are inevitable. The beauty lies in how you weather them. If you have experienced storms in your life, you get what I'm saying. If you haven't, just know you will. Faith prepares you for these storms, and faith will also sustain you until they pass.

Faith is ephemeral. Sometimes you notice its absence more than its presence. You can have faith in your family, yourself, in God, in your decision-making, and in circumstances. For example, I have faith in Phil every day; as long as he's physically and mentally able, he is going to do a great job at Henderson Properties. I'm certain of that, based on his work ethic, his beliefs, and his intelligence. If he has a bad day and loses a client, that doesn't make me lose faith in him. His dedication remains, and that's what I have faith in. Faith is something that you're certain of, but you can't see.

> *If he has a bad day and loses a client, that doesn't make me lose faith in him. His dedication remains, and that's what I have faith in.*

## FAITH AT HOME

Phil and I have chosen to have faith, because we see the difference it makes to those around us, especially to our children. Our faith has defined our family's values, even down to how we schedule our time. For example, when Blake started playing hockey in the fourth grade, ice time in Charlotte was a rare commodity. We often had to play hockey early on Sunday mornings, which made it difficult to get home and get ready for church; but we did it because it was important to us. When we moved to a new home across town, we made finding a new church a priority for our family. We found a non-denominational Christian church nearby. After the first visit, Blake came running out of Sunday school saying, "I don't care if I have to get dressed up every day, I love it here!" It has remained our church home ever since.

The church and our faith have become our family's foundation. When Blake complained in the ninth grade of having to sit in church with us, I simply said, "You have a choice: you can sit with us or go down to the children's room to volunteer. There is always a need." He decided the following week to volunteer, and he spent the next four years teaching Sunday school to children. His younger brother, Grant, followed in his footsteps. I'm not quite sure how much biblical doctrine was taught, but I know my boys learned the value of helping others and being held accountable. Everything starts at home. To this day, my boys send me texts asking me to pray for them or for a friend in need. I am proud of the foundation we have laid for our family, and it gives me great joy and peace to see my sons laying those same foundations in their own lives.

Our shared faith has also helped shape our family's rules and has given us the confidence to abide by those rules even if it's not the norm. For example, we didn't allow our boys to have cell phones until middle-school graduation. They went to a private school and they were the only ones in their grades without cell phones. Despite their occasional protests, we thought they were better for it. Being a kid is hard at times, but being a parent is harder. People talk. People have opinions. As a parent, I second guessed myself a lot. Word got around that our kids didn't have cell phones, that we lived in a nice house, and we expected them to cut the grass, unload the dishwasher, and take out the trash. Oh, the horror! We might have questioned our firm stance on the matter except for our faith in our foundation. It often provides a compass with which to navigate the highs and lows of parenting.

The boys started mowing the yards of our personal rental properties when they were eight and ten years old. Grant, at eight, could barely see over the lawnmower handles. Phil supervised, and it became a Saturday tradition during mowing season. Saturdays were spent playing Pop Warner football with Phil as their coach, mowing together, and then enjoying lunch at a local dive. When Blake went off to college, I think they were sad to lose this father/brother tradition. I would've doubted our ways of raising our kids if it weren't for my faith. Our values became expectations, and therefore, we always held our boys accountable. If there was trouble, there were consequences. If they fought with each other, I made the world stop until they could hug and be friends. With their mowing income they were both able to purchase vehicles when they turned sixteen. They will always remember that accomplishment, and I will always remember seeing the looks of pride on their faces when they were able to earn something through diligence and hard work.

Having faith in your family, yourself, your values, and in something higher adds richness and meaning to your life. We have a rule, for instance, that there are no cell phones at the dinner table. We value our time together—

*Having faith in your family, yourself, your values, and in something higher adds richness and meaning to your life.*

and a meal doesn't last that long, anyway. This rule (which has now become a great habit) allows our family a daily occasion to talk with one another. I'm not going to sugarcoat things—we don't always have deep conversations. But the opportunity is there. It's important to Phil and me that the chance exists, whether it's taken advantage of or not. One cannot be engaged in two things at once such as texting and talking. Recently, over a family dinner, Blake began recounting a day at a second summer job he had in uptown Charlotte. He had been working nights and had befriended a homeless man named Rufus, who sometimes helped him clean at the end of a shift. Blake told us of the conversations they shared—about Rufus' struggle to find a job, his spending habits, and even God. As we had more family dinners, Blake talked more about Rufus and their burgeoning friendship. I began to see a quality in my son I had not seen before: he had a passion for helping the underserved. Blake, who always carries Gatorade with him in case of a low blood sugar, began taking extra bottles with him to share with Rufus. He sometimes offered his tip money to Rufus and continued to encourage his new friend to find a job and turn his life around. Hearing this relationship unfold over the dinner-table conversations made me proud. I was catching the mundane stories of my child's day, but it was so much more than that. He was discovering something about himself. When I told him how proud I was of him for his interest in helping the homeless, I said, "I didn't know that about you." He responded, "I didn't really know it about myself either." If our heads were buried in texts and social media at the table, we might have missed that.

Faith has also helped me accept my children for who they are at all stages of their lives. Children can't be good at everything, but they can be successful in a lot of things. It's important that children know they have important roles at home—ones that are unique to them—so that when they go out into the workplace or college life they feel confident in themselves and what they can offer. Parents must take the time to consider their children's strengths and weaknesses. The hardest part of parenting is letting them be who they are without comparing them to their peers. My children's strengths lie in their personalities, work ethics, and extracurricular activities. My sons weren't at the top of their classes academically. They went to a private school and never took an advanced-placement (AP) course. I will always be grateful to the upper-school dean who once told me, "Please don't put your child in an AP class. Let him succeed where he is supposed to." How about that?

Academic success is important. Don't misunderstand. Phil and I are college grads, and our boys graduated from a college preparatory high school and are both doing well in college. We take education seriously but being book smart is not a prerequisite to success (although, admittedly, it does allow for more options and further education). Leadership and professionalism require skills with budgeting money, risk assessment, and goal setting. Someone with a 4.0 grade-point average (GPA) is smart, that is a fact, even though he or she may have to work hard to maintain that goal. A high GPA will give a person options for college and graduate school, and perhaps help acquire a job out of college, but what happens after that? In the work world the C students typically manage the A students, or so they say. As parents and professional leaders, in my opinion, we shouldn't put

> *As parents and professional leaders, in my opinion, we shouldn't put all the emphasis on GPA scores. The most successful people I know are not the ones who had a 4.0 in high school or college.*

all the emphasis on GPA scores. The most successful people I know are not the ones who had a 4.0 in high school or college. They are the ones who have a strong work ethic, quality leadership skills, and the confidence where needed to take risks.

My faith in my children and their individual paths has helped me realize that not everyone is supposed to be in charge—some lead, others follow. Those lessons are just as important as those learned in the classroom. When Blake was thirteen, for example, he asked what kind of car we were buying him. He didn't get an energetic reply. When he asked again a year or so later, and Phil told him that he'd get whatever he could afford with his saved money from mowing lawns. That Saturday mowing business took on a whole new meaning! Don't be afraid to let your kids see the value of a dollar. Let them make mistakes and endure the consequences. Those are the priceless lessons that will benefit them later in life. I used to feel when my boys made a mistake that I had too. That somehow my parenting skills were thwarted or that I didn't do this or didn't do that. I realized that the "mistakes" are really lessons learned and with those life lessons, as one friend and I like to call them, they will come out wiser and better for it. Embrace the opportunities to teach your children right from wrong and to share meaningful conversations. Do not, however, assume that great grades equal perfect kids who do no wrong and follow all the rules. If you assume that to be true, you will be sadly devastated when they fail.

Little kids equal little problems; big kids equal big problems. I accepted my journey of parenthood with open arms, giving it all I had. Enjoy the journey of parenting and mentorship, but make it yours with no fear of regret that you should've, would've, or could've. Love them for who they are as individuals, make sure they under-stand your expectations and what your family stands for, celebrate their strengths, coach them accordingly, and always keep in mind that your dreams may not be theirs.

As a parent of two college students, I'll tell you that kids grow up and time passes quickly. When it's time for your children to leave the nest, they'll need two things: roots and wings—roots that ground them and bind them to you and wings to fly solo. Roots only attach if watered and wings only spread if given room. Don't forget to have your own plan, so that when your kids fly solo, you might find your wings, too. For Phil and me, our journey isn't over. We are helping the boys navigate through the college years and enjoying living vicariously through them. It's a privilege and joy seeing them mature and find their own way at this stage.

---

## IF YOU HAVE CHILDREN, YOUNG OR OLD, THERE ARE SEVERAL THINGS THAT YOU CAN DO TO CULTIVATE FAITH AND SHARED VALUES WITHIN YOUR HOME:

- Write a family mission statement and hang it in your house.

- Have your kids plan your next vacation. You'll be amazed at what they can do.

- Give a child one chore to do each week and hold him or her accountable.

- Be vocal about your personal goals and your family's shared goals. Don't forget to point out when those goals have been accomplished. Celebrate fulfilled goals as important achievements for your family.

- Find a church and attend as often as possible. Our Sundays are now a tradition when the boys are home from school.

- Provide opportunities for your child to talk to you and have your undivided attention. That means put all screens away.

---

## FAITH IN BUSINESS

Faith has been the driving force throughout the life of Henderson Properties. Without it, I'm not certain we would've succeeded. For Phil and me, faith includes a Biblical component, but it also means having faith in ourselves, in each other, and in the business that we started from scratch. I couldn't have made Henderson Properties what it is today without Phil, and I'm confident he would say the same thing. Faith also includes having faith in our work team. Now that our team has been built, faith allows us to trust in those people and the care that we put into selecting them. Faith in ourselves, each other, and in something greater, helps us stay calm and focused. Putting faith out in front of everything we do gives us purpose and puts things in perspective.

Our faith has carried us through many storms, but it has also created some of its own. As entrepreneurs, our faith has been used against us at times. Mainly it's been used to swindle more vacation time or to criticize Phil when he made an unpopular decision. What is the point of bringing someone down in front of others? This is where my Christian faith comes into play. No one is perfect. However, I know that I want to treat people with grace and mercy. Looking up toward the heavens is so much better than looking down. Trust me, I've tried it both ways.

I tell you this because being an entrepreneur means you will be tested, and you will struggle at times. Some days will be harder than others. That's life. Whether you are an entrepreneur, manager, employee, or parent, you need affirmation and strength, which can come from focusing on something larger than yourself. You need somewhere, someone, or something to turn to. Accepting the journey of entrepreneurship came easy for Phil and me. We thought we knew what we were getting into when we raised a glass to entrepreneurship on our honeymoon. The truth, however, is that we didn't really know. We weren't prepared for the unforeseen challenges of interpersonal relationships with staff. Spoiler alert: people aren't always nice! As the leader of the business, you often have to make unpopular decisions; being the leader also means you hold space for your staff's feedback. You need faith and convictions to ground you and hold you firmly in place, otherwise, it is difficult not to take some feedback personally.

Recently I was on my way to the grocery store listening to a radio interview with a Carolina Panthers football player who said defensive players win games. I was intrigued. I, like most people, would have said that quarterbacks and wide receivers—the offensive players—win games. This player, however, was saying that the defense is on guard and stops the offense. He went on to say these players are strong in their stances, in their positions. They have faith in themselves and in their teammates. He said life is

> *As the leader of the business, you often have to make unpopular decisions; being the leader also means you hold space for your staff's feedback.*

the same way. He noted how faith gives you the courage and strength to get through the tough times. The same principle holds true in business—people who are full of faith and positivity are not limited by fear of failure, because even if they fail, they are firmly rooted in their foundation.

I can unequivocally repeat that I could not have built a family or a business without my faith. The birth of my children and the subsequent birth of Henderson Properties was the beginning of my adventure, but it was my faith that allowed me to settle in and truly accept my journey. I was able to embrace the good times and the bad times, because my faith gave me something bigger and more powerful to look toward. Regardless of our faith, our family status, or our professional training, we all have journeys. We will be tossed about in the storms of life, and without faith it might not seem worth it—but with faith at the helm, we can accept all of the beauty and lessons the journey has to offer.

## ON FAITH

### by Phil Henderson

Having faith in God has been a central theme of my adult life and has guided me in my family life, my marriage, and my business. Having faith includes knowing that God is in control, no matter the situation. Having faith also allows a business owner to take the risks necessary to grow the business. If you have faith in your team and confidence that God will provide for you, it makes even the riskiest decisions a lot easier.

Being a business owner means that you make multiple decisions every day that affect the lives of the people around you. Some of these choices are small ones, but they can still be critical to the success of your business. I used to worry a lot about various aspects of our business, such as losing customers, employee retention, increased medical-insurance costs, the list goes on and on. Having faith does not remove these stressors, but it reminds me there is something bigger at work. Over the years I've found myself praying more and more and asking God for wisdom. I make it a practice to pray for guidance in all the decisions I make at Henderson Properties. This doesn't guarantee that all my choices are the correct ones, but I feel confident that I'm making judgements that are in line with our company's core values and vision statement.

For example, when we have an opening at Henderson Properties, I pray that God will send us the right person—someone who can help further our company's mission. As a growing business we are constantly recruiting to keep up with the expansion. Getting the right people on our team is critical, and I know that God makes much better hiring decisions than I do. This allows me to hire staff confidently and then have faith in our Henderson Properties team. I know that all team members are doing their best to provide the real estate services that positively affect the quality of people's lives every day. Our team works hard to fulfill our obligations to our clients, whether it's our community association managers overseeing the beautification of a community that we manage, or one of our Realtors helping one of our buyers find the home of their dreams. Our management team, which consists of all our division managers, is responsible for setting our quarterly and annual goals, and I have faith in them and their tireless efforts and commitments.

My faith also allows me to be a stronger, more confident leader. My leadership style has always been one of leading by example. I try to set a good example for our team with my work ethic and character. I've never been much of a "cheerleader" type. (I leave that up to Shelly.) My faith also keeps me humble, because I know that God is responsible for the intelligence I have been gifted with as well as the success of my personal and professional life. I'm humbled and grateful that God has put me in the position I'm in. I am so proud of the life and the business that Shelly and I started from scratch. We have been blessed in many ways—yet I have faith that our greatest accomplishments with Henderson Properties are still to come!

---

## HENDERSON PROPERTIES EMPLOYEE SPOTLIGHT:

*When I first started with Henderson in June 2014, I was very nervous and quiet. I wasn't sure how people would perceive me, if they would like me, or how they would take my funny (or what I believe is funny) sense of humor. Eventually, I started making friends and started being invited out to birthday lunches for employees in different departments. At that point, I knew that I was starting to fit in. I knew these new friends had actually become my work family.*

*In May 2015, I was being tested for a lump under my arm and four large masses in my stomach. Not knowing what they were or where this journey might take me, I put my faith in God but also shared my concerns with a few of my coworkers. I ended up being scheduled for surgery in August of that year for removal of the masses. During that trying time, I realized my coworkers were more than that and that*

*Henderson Properties was not just my employer. I realized they were my Charlotte family.*

*During my surgery, my coworkers sent out an e-mail to the whole company asking them to lift me up in prayers. They also appointed one of them to keep in constant contact with my husband during my surgery. During my recovery, I received the most beautiful peace lily (my favorite) delivered to my door with a card read "Best wishes for a speedy recovery! We all miss you around the office." It was signed "Your Henderson Properties Work Family." When I read it, I teared up (of course) and told my mom that I had finally found where I belonged!*

*Thank you,*

**KRYSTAL YORK ROGERS**

*Community Association Manager*

---------------------------------------------------------

# CHAPTER 8

- - - - - - - - - - - - - - - - - - - - - - - - - - -

# PEOPLE FIRST

*I can't believe God put us on this earth to be ordinary.*

## — LOU HOLTZ

lot has changed over the years at Henderson Properties. For instance, our babies have grown into young
men, our small staff has increased to a team of sixty,
our office space has expanded, and our leadership styles
have evolved. With so many changes, it would be easy to approach
our business legacy like a hummingbird, darting from one detail to
another, trying to fit together all the discordant elements. Phil and I
don't feel as though the key to our success is in those details. It's in the
*foundation* that we laid decades ago. Despite all the changes over the
life of our business, there are some things that have never changed
for Henderson Properties—like the mission of the company and our
belief in ourselves and our staff.

Our Henderson Properties vision statement is one that we take seriously and commit to daily: Providing real estate services that positively affect the quality of people's lives, every day. In choosing the right people, we can further our vision and create a more solid foundation on which to build. Work/life balance can be a real challenge, but if we commit to attempting to create balance, then even if we fall short, we're moving in the right direction to make things better. When we planned for the future of Henderson Properties using this vision, we saw more success. We wanted the future to be about others and not so much about ourselves and what we thought was best for Henderson Properties. We realized that if we personally and professionally supported others, we would all grow and evolve.

*Providing real estate services that positively affect the quality of people's lives, every day.*

Our company vision statement was drafted based on faith in ourselves, our team, and the foundation we laid early on. We have a staff that genuinely commits to excellence in everything they do. We want to foster that in the office and in the homes of our team; we want to positively impact everyone we encounter. When you commit to something, you have a calm determination to see it through. That does not mean, however, that you mentally set a goal and then surrender to whatever happens. You must build a solid foundation first. You must get the right training, hire good people, set appropriate goals, build a support system, and then you must have confidence in those choices.

---------------------------------------------------------------

## AT HENDERSON PROPERTIES, OUR SHARED VALUES INCLUDE:

- Providing support and availability to meet clients' expectations.

- Demonstrating honest and ethical behavior in all business transactions.

- Promoting a positive life balance environment.

- Committing to excellence in everything we do.

Shared values are the fundamental beliefs, concepts, and principles that underline the culture of an organization, and which guide decisions and behavior of its employees and management alike. Shared values are just that—shared by all.

Having successful communication with staff creates a healthy business culture. Leaders must not only create the vision and goals but effectively communicate them to the staff. Every company has a culture, and it all starts with the brand. The brand starts with the employees. What they say, how they act, and how they treat the customer is what makes the brand. When that brand and expectation is shared, the staff knows what the goal is.

We strive daily to instill these shared values that we have provided to our staff. We do that by hiring the right people and then training them to do a job well done. We don't expect perfection, but we always strive to be the best we can be.

---------------------------------------------------------------

## HENDERSON PROPERTIES CORE VALUES:

- We are prepared.

- We actively listen and communicate well with clients and employees.
- We strategically prioritize our initiatives.
- We empower our employees.
- We make decisions in a timely manner.

-------------------------------------------------------------

As of this writing, we own the office building that houses Henderson Properties. We used to fit comfortably in the space. Eventually we became snugly tucked in, and now we are frankly too close for comfort. This is a wonderful problem to have, but the growing pains are noticeable. In 2015, I began helping with the office-expansion project and was in charge of finding an architect. We thought adding onto our current building sounded better than uprooting computers, cubicles, phone lines, and people. We had prayed that this was what we should do and felt confident in our decision; we even shared our architect plans, including start and end dates, with our staff. About eighteen months into the project—after many meetings with the architect and city government zoning personnel—we discovered that our second parking lot, which would be the foundation for our new building, was sand. That meant that before we could even begin building, we would need to spend thousands of dollars to shore up the foundation. That was a frustrating day, but the lesson was clear—you cannot build on a weak foundation. The day after we decided to cancel the building project, a wonderful office space went up for sale with almost three times the space, costing us about the same as the renovation. The new office offers a corner lot, trees, picnic area, full kitchen,

-----------------------------------

*The lesson was clear— you cannot build on a weak foundation.*

-----------------------------------

and a lot of space for growth. We made an offer, and it was accepted. Coincidence? I think not! This upcoming move is going to bring a few challenges with it, but it's going to be worth it, because we're moving to a bigger and better space that will provide new opportunities for people to come work and grow with us.

Our building-expansion fiasco provides an apt metaphor for the importance of establishing a foundation for your business. The mission statements and values are not details; they are the foundation. Our business has been built on principles we believe in and have stood for. With every decision we make, we recommit to excellence. One way we extend this to our staff and our community is by putting people first. *People First* started out as a theme at Henderson Properties for 2017, but it was so powerful throughout the company that we have adopted it long-term. One way we incorporate *People First* around our staff is fun and simple: we start each year with an annual meeting at an off-site location. We have a full day of recapping the previous year's goals, presenting the new year's goals, celebrating the successes, and talking about what the future holds. It's very important to present the plan to our staff. If we say it out loud, put it in writing, and commit to it, then we are all focused on the same successful outcome. Just like the defensive lineman who is focused on his one opponent, everyone has a shared goal and understands the expectations for the new year.

At a recent staff meeting, we discussed the theme of gratitude and decided to make it our focus. I gave all employees a notecard with one word written on it: *gratitude.* I told them to place the card in a visible spot and each time they looked at it, think of something they are grateful for at work or at home. In the weeks following this simple exercise, both men and women in the office sent me photos of their cards tucked into various places—beside their desk, tacked on a wall, propped beside a plant. One of the maintenance workers sent me a message that read, "Shelly, I don't have a desk at the office, but here's my *gratitude* card in my office van." He attached a photo of his *gratitude* card propped on his dashboard. I appreciate having a staff that is so willing to adjust their mind-sets, thereby changing the lives of the people around us, our community, and our families. You can see it in their positivity; you can see it when they walk through the door each day. They're the ones who are sharing the gratitude. Being an entrepreneur means that you not only get the satisfaction of building something; you also get the satisfaction of forming a team that creates a positive message and shares it with many.

Success does not happen in a vacuum. Rewards compound when they're shared with others. As we grow and add to our staff, it's important that we try to create a workplace that is conducive and holds true to these principles. We have become diligent about whom we hire. Will they hold space for our shared values and commit to excellence? I cannot prove that rewards increase when shared with others, but I know it to be true—because I've lived it. Phil and I commit to this game-changing approach to business building by giving employees opportunities to grow, to do community service, to spend time with their families, to apply for in-house promotions, and to participate in paid continuing-education training. When employees see that an employer is engaged in the company, one of the rewards is that we can celebrate their individual successes. One of the ways that we do that at Henderson Properties is through our monthly staff meetings. These meetings are geared toward keeping the staff informed, motivated, and engaged in celebrating one another's professional successes. One of the greatest benefits of building a business is acknowledging the team and all they have contributed to the company. We are so grateful to have such a strong group of individuals, and we hope that by making *People First* a guiding principle of Henderson Properties, we are giving back to a staff of people who have given us so much.

We try to change the game of customer service by applying *People First* to every interaction we have with clients. We put our customers first by educating new board members through a new-board-member orientation. We also take the time to educate and support prospective tenants who get approved to rent a home. We inform each new tenant about the expectations concerning rent payment, due dates, payment submissions, and late-payment penalties.

Phil and I are confident in the foundation of Henderson Properties that we've spent so many years building. If not for our confidence in that foundation and the shared commitments of our staff, we would be up pacing every night. We'd have so many tiny details to sweat over that we wouldn't be able to enjoy this life that we have built from scratch. It is important for entrepreneurs to identify your values and then align your businesses with those. Incorporating your values and beliefs in your business may be easier than you think, because you're probably doing this more than you realize. Find something you believe in, stand up for it at all costs, and then build your foundation on that principle. Make sure you hire people who respect this vision and continue to articulate and circulate these principles to your staff. Have confidence in your business, in your leadership, and in the foundation you've built. If you're just starting out in your business, take the time to build a solid foundation. Make it strong, and then have faith and certainty in what you have built. Don't worry. The ones who don't buy in will ultimately bail out.

## BUILDING A STRONG FOUNDATION IN YOUR WORKPLACE:

- Identify your values.
- Create a vision statement based on those values.
- Make sure your coworkers/employees understand and commit to the vision statement .
- Change your workplace to be conducive to your values and beliefs.
- Encourage staff to participate in community events by offering time off or other incentives.
- Make opportunities for staff to participate in team building.
- Make people a priority.
- Find joy by doing meaningful things with meaningful people—this includes your team at work .
- Find a support network of other employees/entrepreneurs who share your values and are interested in sharing ways to incorporate them into the workplace .
- Try and fail—that's when you evolve, as you realize your strengths and weaknesses.
- Commit to these values, then let every decision you make be informed by and built on this foundation.

For Phil and me, much of our energies have been spent applying *People First* to our employees, clients, and business partners. It wasn't until about 2013 or so that we realized that *People First* sometimes means *us*. The saying "When mama's not happy, no one is happy" holds true for a business owner, too. At times we have put so much emphasis and energy on the company and making employees happy that we forgot about what makes us happy.

Building a successful business is not as revolutionary as building one that truly cares about people. We wanted Henderson Properties to offer our staff and our customers something that wasn't offered elsewhere. We wanted to offer a company with a heart where people come first. We wanted to humanize the business world. We wanted our personal core values to match our company's core values. We wanted to create an environment where people are encouraged and rewarded for having a positive mindset. We didn't set out to do this at first, but it has unfolded as we held true to our principles, values, and goals. If we can do that, then we have changed our workplace, we have changed the homes of our employees, we have affected their children, and without sounding too lofty, we have at least attempted to make the world a more positive place. For too long, we have used our brains at work and our hearts at home. My hope is to encourage others to bring their hearts into the conference room. Don't leave them behind. Let them guide you, motivate you, and be the foundation on which you build.

-------------------------------------------------------

## HENDERSON PROPERTIES EMPLOYEE SPOTLIGHT:

*I had previously worked for Henderson Properties for more than three years. This was the first real job I had after moving to Charlotte, and I was welcomed by everyone with open arms. They accepted me for who I was, helped me grow as a person and employee, and became my work family. The relationships I built made it incredibly difficult to leave, but I felt I needed to at that time. I never wanted to leave and was fearful I would never be able to return. Thanks to Stacey Gillespie, Phil, and Shelly, I was able to.*

*I am often asked why did I come back. The answer is simple: I came back to my work home and family. No company, job, or person is perfect. If anyone is looking for that, they may be looking for a long time. What is perfect to me is understanding what is important and finding the place that best fits within that. It's important to have the support of my supervisor; to be able to be myself no matter how silly or hyper I'm feeling; to have people around me who care for me and my well-being; and to have an opinion I can share without fear of repercussions. My life is better because of the opportunities and people I have met at Henderson Properties, and for this, I am truly grateful.*

**STELLA JALON**
*Community-Association Manager*

--------------------------------------------------------

## HENDERSON PROPERTIES
## EMPLOYEE SPOTLIGHT:

*Since I joined Henderson Properties in 1999, the company has grown, the children have grown up, and we have all grown older (and wiser, I hope). As I write this, it's four years since I retired from Henderson Properties, but I keep coming back—whenever and wherever there's a spot for me. I just celebrated my one-year anniversary ... again! Retirement is great, but there are only so many books to read, cakes to bake, and people to visit.*

*I am so thankful for the opportunity to be a part of Henderson Properties—a company that has created a legacy for itself. Over the years, many things have changed, but there is one thing that has not changed, and I don't think it ever will: whether five employees, fifty employees, or five hundred employees, Henderson Properties is family. Always has been, always will be.*

**SANDY SMITH**
*Administrative Support Specialist*

---------------------------------------------------------

# CHAPTER 9

------------------------------

# GAME CHANGER

*As we look ahead into the next century, leaders*
*will be those who empower others.*

**— BILL GATES**

uring my adolescent golfing days in the early '80s, boys dominated the sports world. Male athletes got much of the scholarship money, uniform budgets, and opportunities to play in a variety of sports. It didn't occur to me at the time that this was any kind of hardship. It was just the way things were. It was only when I became an entrepreneur that I thought back to my sports training and considered its effect on me. As a female entrepreneur at the start of Henderson Properties, I was again a minority. There were rarely other women in the business groups we joined; there weren't many books or training classes for women in business; there was no support group to help navigate the intricacies of a work/life balance. If you wanted to read up on the subject you pretty much had to go to the library. True to my personality, this didn't bother me, it was simply how it was. I think my generation accepted life for what it was at the time. We didn't know any better but that is not to say life wasn't good then. It seemed simpler. In fact, it reminded me of competing in sports, and I often found myself playing "with the boys" in the conference room, as I had on the golf course.

With the birth of Henderson Properties, I didn't set out to be a renegade. Well, maybe I *did* have something to prove. Some entrepreneurs have to prove they can do it on their own with each having their own motivating factor. My father thought it was on the golf course, but just maybe it was at the office. Looking back, I have come to realize that being a female entrepreneur at the time probably was a pretty big deal. I was just making decisions to further my professional development and provide for my family. I was focused, not on changing the world or on changing any type of gender roles; I simply wanted to make a difference one day for my family, my community, and the business we were building. I felt strongly about our efforts and what could be if we succeeded. I think those motivations are the same for men and women, and in this way, entrepreneurship is the great leveler. As entrepreneurs there is no pressure of salary or benefits—because, as the business owner, what you earn is up to you. Though keep in mind that in the beginning you won't be the highest-paid employee. The business world today is still male dominated. It's a fact, and I don't have a problem with that. Why? Because I've proven my point that with hard work and dependability on oneself, along with some faith and vision, any woman can achieve remarkable things. Don't depend on others to turn the tide. *You* go out there and do it! And—whether or not your goal is to revolutionize the world— just lead where you are!

## LUNCH & LEARN BOOK CLUB

As a female entrepreneur, I have been given a unique platform to reach others in a positive way.

It is my goal to lead others where they are. I created my Tuesday Group "Lunch & Learn" book club as a way to engage with other employees and empower them to become better both personally and professionally. (It was probably more for me, truth be told, as I was looking for ways to better myself.) In the ten-week Lunch and Learn courses at Henderson Properties, I invite employees to join me in reading books that further their professional development and to join me in ongoing conversations about leadership. In these training courses, we discuss topics like how to be happy, how to be a leader when you don't feel like one, how to improve office culture, and how to manage a work/life balance. The book and lunch are provided by me at bi-weekly meetings where we discuss the different topics and how we can implement them into our work and daily lives.

There are a number of inspirational books that can help transform our thinking and stop self-defeating thoughts and habits. My two favorite titles thus far have been *The 360 Degree Leader* by Max Lucado and *The Happiness Advantage* by Shawn Anchor.

Taking this time with my team allows us to become more engaged in each other's lives. It creates a sense of community and connection in our work environment. The series has grown each time I offer the course, and I think it has created a deep mutual respect between everyone involved. With so much negativity in the world, I feel called to spread some joy in my own corner. Where better to start than with Henderson Properties? When people feel appreciated and strong, they perform well. We want to cultivate team players who have a desire to grow and empower others.

## LEADERSHIP PROGRAM

As a way of taking that group a step further, in 2018 I rolled out our first-ever "Leadership Program," where we take two to three volunteer candidates twice a year and we mentor and coach them to become future leaders of our company. It is a program designed for individuals who want a long-term career and not just a "job" within our company. This is yet another way to show our "people-first" and "shared-value" focus.

One of the most powerful motivations of my leadership-training courses is to reframe how a person views his or her hardships. The new trainees I meet with for leadership classes are a varied bunch. There are men and women, some younger, some older, from different socio-economic backgrounds and religious beliefs, but there are some aspects of their lives that are universal. One of those is hardship. We have all weathered storms, some more tumultuous than others. Some of these storms happened long ago, but they still haunt us; others are happening in the present and altering our outlook on the future. These crises can be financial, personal, medical, mental, or professional. Some are bigger than others, but they are all valid. The basic question I ask in my leadership-training courses is: *Do hardships have to define us? Do they have to limit us?*

When I was in college, my parents separated and ultimately divorced. I was blindsided. The dissolution of my home shook my own identity, and I found myself at a crossroads. My family unit seemed broken, just as I was about to graduate college. What was I going to do with my life? As with many of life's hardships, this one forged my personality in unexpected ways. My father was a business owner as well, but his empire crumbled because of his poor decision making and life choices. I got an early lesson in the ways one's thoughts and feelings in personal life can bleed over into the professional realm. Most humans are not as good at compartmentalizing as we like to think. We all make mistakes and go through difficult times. Making mistakes is human; fixing them and learning from them is evolution. Because of my father's choices and their impacts on my family, I could clearly see the principles that would define my future. I wanted to live my life with integrity, and I wanted to make a difference in the world for the good of other people. I wanted my family to be proud of me. I

> *I got an early lesson in the ways one's thoughts and feelings in personal life can bleed over into the professional realm. Most humans are not as good at compartmentalizing as we like to think.*

wanted people around me to be happy. I wanted to do things the right way. I did not want hardships from my past to limit my future. While I would never have chosen those unhappy circumstances, I now realize that—as hard as they were—they ultimately helped change my life for the better. These principles would become the driving force behind every decision I'd make in life, both at home and at the office. Some entrepreneurs have a past story that has motivated them to want to do things differently or better. I think this steadfastness is one of the things that makes Henderson Properties so unique and is changing the game of business leadership. If there is a past circumstance that *you* are carrying, please dump it; let it go. Give thanks for it and be done. Your past doesn't define you. (See the Resources section at the end of the book for additional tools to develop your leadership skills.)

Our Henderson Properties story is only one of many entrepreneurial success stories. Ours isn't necessarily better than anyone else's, but it is unique and special to us. We never had the goal of being the biggest company in Charlotte, but we do strive to be the best. We have built an exceptional business that we think is changing the game of business models in our area. I wrote this book because I felt I had a story to tell, and an opportunity presented itself. Opportunity creates growth whether personal or professional. Even if you aren't looking to start a business, you can become a valuable employee, a better leader, and a more fulfilled person. Whether you lead a team of one or one hundred, it's time to talk about how you can change your mind-set and, thus, change the game. Here's how:

**BE MOTIVATED**. Motivation is a state of mind that is essential for success. Entrepreneurs often have stories of moving from rags to riches. They sometimes come from humble beginnings. Perhaps when someone doesn't have much, he or she works even harder. Same as in parenting: We often want to give our kids the world if we are able, but what does that really teach them? It certainly doesn't teach them motivation. If we can have everything we want at our disposal, there is no motivation to work hard. Motivation is what gets you out there. Motivation predicts success better than intelligence or ability, which is the reason why a lot of A students are managed by the C students. At Henderson Properties, we don't set out necessarily to hire the top of the class. Neither Phil nor I graduated college with honors, but we did work for our grades and graduated from Appalachian State University with valuable teamwork and leadership skills. When we are hiring, we aren't focused on A students, as much as we are seeking A players. We are interested in a person's willingness, integrity, and motivation. Can you make the business better by being a part of it? Do you have what it takes to be a team player? We are all motivated by different rewards and outcomes. Figure out what motivates you and go after it. Once you know yourself better, you can reap the benefits of success in all areas of your life.

**FIND YOUR PURPOSE AT ANY AGE.** There is no *perfect* age to start a business. Phil and I were thirty-five and thirty-three years old when we started Henderson Properties. And trust me when I say there is never a perfect time to start a business, either. Life, money, kids, all get in the way. There will always be obstacles. You will get knocked down. We started Henderson Properties for us, not for anyone else. We knew the timing wasn't the most ideal, with two small children and no financial backing, but we wanted to be our own bosses. We saw an opportunity and we took a chance. That's how many successful entrepreneurs' stories begin.

**FIND THE BEAUTY.** What is standing in your way today? Life is full of so much beauty and joy. Sometimes we must dig deep to find it. Other times we are struck by the beauty and purity of experience, and those moments can sustain us for days, weeks, or months. Finding the sacred in the mundane is a skill, and like any skill, it must be practiced to be strengthened. Stay focused on what is good and beautiful in your life. Don't let circumstances and past failures get the best of you. Keep a gratitude journal or make it a daily practice to list five things of beauty that you saw, felt, or experienced until it becomes habit.

**ALWAYS LOOK FOR THE OPPORTUNITIES IN YOUR LIFE.** Try to meet new people, take risks, try a new hobby, attend a seminar to better yourself. You never know what lies in your future or who you may meet unless you get out there. The older we get, the more challenging it is to step outside of what we know. We get lazy; we get comfortable. You must be self-motivated to resist this apathy, because where there is motivation, there is opportunity. One is never too old to learn if the desire is there. My grandmother lived to one hundred years old, in large part because she had the motivation and desire to live a full life rather than "sit in the rocking chair and knit a sweater," as she used to say. You will notice that as you look for opportunities, more of them appear. Cultivate this mind-set and you will find that each day brings new promise.

**LEAD AND INSPIRE OTHERS**. If you are currently in a leadership position, you have a platform and daily opportunities to inspire and encourage the people around you. At Henderson Properties, we set out to positively affect the lives of our staff and clients every day. We use this platform to help others and are ourselves motivated to inspire change through our company, our community, and our world. For example, each year, we host a Second Harvest Food Bank canned-food drive with our participating HOAs. Last year, we collected over two thousand pounds of canned goods to donate to the homeless and underserved members of our community. In addition, we give one paid day off a year for our staff to volunteer at a charity, church, or school of their choosing. We also offer two paid summer internships to prospective college students who are interested in learning more about the aspects of real estate. Our platform is as large as we dare to make it.

It is important to me to pay it forward because I feel like to whom much is given, much is required. Mentoring others is one of the most profound things I do. In my leadership courses, I encourage attendees to give back to the people around them. No matter who you are or what you've experienced, there is someone out there who can benefit from what you've learned. What a beautiful way to pay it forward. This can add value to your failures and recast your hardships into powerful tools that are catalysts for the transformation of others. I want people to have what I have. I don't think entrepreneurs are envious or jealous people. Most entrepreneurs who have started from scratch, like Phil and myself, have been on the other side of the hiring table. I've been the employee. I've lived in a thousand-square-foot home. I've eaten Hamburger Helper for dinner when we couldn't afford anything else. I've been there. I've done it. I have had the opportunity to learn so many lessons in my life, and I feel it's my responsibility and my honor to share whatever knowledge I have with others.

----------------------------------------------------------------

**FOR THE SOLE ENTREPRENEUR**: Even if you are a sole entrepreneur with no partner to share the rewards with, you will still benefit from your business in ways greater and more fulfilling than profit and expansion. You will gain self-understanding. Whether or not your business succeeds, you can still take pride in your effort. It is incredibly fulfilling to build something from nothing. It is a creative endeavor much like raising children, writing a book, or building a house. It all starts with a mental concept, and then it becomes a physical reality. You get to be the creator of something, and there is great power in that. In addition, you get to contribute to the lives of your staff, and you get to infuse your community and your industry with positivity and graciousness. These are no small feats. These are the ways we can change the game and the world.

**FOR THE YOUNG WANNABE ENTREPRENEUR**: What are you waiting for? Everyone has the same amount of time each day. Use your time wisely. Surround yourself with the right people and just go for it. People are so often intimidated by young people. In my first year of teaching school, for example, I had several parents say, "It's your first year as a teacher, you don't have any experience." I never really had a comeback to that. I've realized, in my time spent hiring for Henderson Properties, that young people might lack experience, but they also lack a fear of failure. If they've not failed, they don't know failure, and they don't fear it. It's a powerful perspective to work from a place that is not rooted in fear. The young people are energetic and optimistic. They're ready to make their mark in society. They have confidence. They are going to rule the world.

**FOR THE SEASONED EMPLOYEE/RETIREE**: Older people are living better-quality lives due to technology and medicine. It's never too late to start your own business, though you might prefer one that's smaller and more manageable. My mother started a pet-sitting business when she was seventy-eight years old. She had business cards printed and circulated them at her neighborhood's business events. She loves animals, and she enjoys having some extra money and the structure it provides to her day. It's important during this season of life to continue to be engaged in a community and to keep doing the things you enjoy. The best medicine is oftentimes feeling like an integral, valued member of one's community. What better way to do that than to offer a service that you enjoy providing? Older people work hard because they're from a generation that works until the job is complete. They're also familiar with failure; therefore, they understand and appreciate success.

**FOR THE STAY-AT-HOME PARENT**: It's your time! Now that your kids are in school or moving out of the house, it's time to find your purpose. It was a sad time when my first son left for college. I didn't know what life was going to look like. But after both my boys were in college, I looked at it differently: while they were doing their thing, Mama was doing hers! Sitting at home is not an option. Figure out what your purpose is, outside of parental duties. What excites you? What are you passionate about? Use all the leadership and time-management skills that you honed while at home with your children and offer them to an existing company—or start your own. Never under-estimate the powerful skills you've been acquiring while home with your children. You can contribute so much to a professional team.

**FOR THE ESTABLISHED ENTREPRENEUR**: Keep chal-lenging yourself and take time to appreciate the people you have in your workplace. Look at your policies and pro-cedures and determine whether you are putting people first. A business that lacks a heart isn't self-sustaining. If you want to keep your employees happy and productive, build a business they can be proud of. If you're successful, pay it forward, put people first, and bring a human element back to the workplace. Dialogue with your employees about their work/life balance. How might you support their efforts? What could you do to open the communi-cation with your team? People might come to a job for a paycheck, but they don't *stay* at a job just for the paycheck. As an entrepreneur/business owner, we have an obliga-tion to the people who work for us to create a challenging, enriching environment for them. This creates an inspiring atmosphere and can have dramatic effects on productivity and attitude.

------------------------------------------------------------

One of the most liberating aspects of entrepreneurship is how personalized it is. You can create a business around whatever niche interests you. You can create a job that perfectly suits your leadership style and interests. The downside, however, is that you also bring your hardships with you. You bring your self-defeating thoughts and behaviors. Owning your own business gives you a quick lesson in how thoughts of failure often lead to a business' demise. It's your life, your obstacles, your opportunities, your business, your game. It is not healthy to live in negativity, and the more you identify with it, the more debilitating it is. We can't blame others for our failures, nor can we procrastinate and dwell on the reasons why something can't be done. When you take the time to face your trials and transform them into personality-building traits, you are changing your life, you are changing the game.

I'm honored to have the opportunity to share what I have learned about my own professional and personal evolution. Each time I have the opportunity to speak to staff during leadership training or to novice entrepreneurs in my community and beyond, I am overwhelmed by the dedication and the determination they show. Entrepreneurs are not the ones who have the world handed to them; they're the ones who build it. I hope I can continue to empower and inspire professionals to go for it. Go for all of it. I often tell attendees in my leadership training courses that the focus shouldn't be on whether you can *have* it all, but on whether you have the confidence and dedication to *make* it all. It's never too late to start building the life you want from scratch.

## HENDERSON PROPERTIES
## EMPLOYEE SPOTLIGHT:

*I was born and raised in such a small town in West Virginia, and I never had the opportunity to travel, so my small town was all I ever knew. When I first moved to Charlotte, I was overwhelmed by the tall buildings, fast interstates, and all the people. Every day during my job search, I thought "With such a big city like this there has to be so many opportunities around every corner!"*

*After about two months, I was called by a temporary employment agency for a job as a community-association manager associate at a company named Henderson Properties. My first thought was, "What is a community-association manager associate?" I had a lot of experience with property management and rentals, but I was new to this. On the day of my interview I remember walking in after battling the traffic, and I was nervous. I was thinking I was a small-town girl and probably wouldn't fit in with a company like this. I walked in the front door and was pleasantly greeted by the front-desk staff, and I was told to take a seat. I believe I must have begun to turn blue from holding my breath, because the woman at the front desk turned to me and said, "Just breath; everything will be okay. You will do great." Suddenly a peace came over me, and I took a deep breath and prepared for my interview. After my interview, I was truly excited about the company. Luckily, I got the position, though I was told that it was only a temporary position and*

*I would only be filling in until the employee returned from medical leave.*

*When I walked through the doors of Henderson Properties on my first day on the job, everyone greeted me with open arms and warm hearts. The company was so diverse with so many different personalities, that I fit right in! I was trained and shown all about HOAs and the company, and my eyes were open to so much more. After a couple of weeks, I was an HOA pro. Henderson Properties had taught me so much.*

*I would walk down the hallway and hear people call, "Hey, Kellie!" To this company I wasn't just another person from a temporary agency or another employee just working in the HOA department—I was a person, an individual. That's when I began to fall in love with Henderson Properties; in this huge city, here is a company that feels like family. The company stood for everything I was looking for in a career. They believed in helping others, putting people first, seeing staff as individuals. They took the extra step to help the home owners, the tenants, and the clients. They were growing, and I could see my future with Henderson Properties. I began to look at this place as somewhere I wanted to be, a company I wanted to be part of. I wanted to be a Henderson Properties employee, and I wanted to be a part of this family. But still I knew my assignment was only temporary.*

*I knew in my heart that I was meant to be here, that Henderson Properties was meant to be a part of my* life. Every day I hoped that they would say, "Welcome to the family, Kellie. You are now an official employee of Henderson Properties!" I would hear stories about how Shelly and Phil first began the company and how much it has grown now. I heard about all the things they did for their employees. I remember walking down the hallway and seeing Mr. Henderson's door wide open. He welcomed staff to come in to say hello anytime. I would watch as managers went in and out to discuss how things were going. He was so willing to help, and he truly cared; we weren't just employees to him. I remember meeting Mrs. Henderson and feeling her warm spirit like a ray of sunshine. She talked with such excitement about wanting to contribute and help. It just seemed so unreal, so unheard of, I just couldn't believe it. They appreciated every single one of their employees, and they didn't just give you a paycheck to show it or a party to prove it, they gave you their time and their willingness to help!

I began to be thankful; even if I didn't become an official employee of Henderson Properties, I still got a chance to really see something remarkable—a company that was more than just a business but a family. I got the opportunity to experience what every company in this world should be like. I saw how this world would be a better place if there were more people like Mr. and Mrs. Henderson running businesses. I can proudly say I am now an official employee of Henderson Properties, and I try my best to contribute every day toward putting people first. I have learned so much with this *company and hope I can give back as much as it has given to me.*

**KELLIE JOHNSON**

*Community Association Manager Associate*

-----------------------------------------------------------

# CONCLUSION:

# THE STORY CONTINUES

At the beginning of Henderson Properties, people told us that we were crazy to start a new business with two small children in tow. We didn't listen. In fact, we never even discussed what would happen if we didn't make it. Even during all the turmoil and the hardships, we never had a backup plan. In preparing for this book, I asked my sons what they remember from those early days of Henderson Properties. I wondered if they remembered being whisked off to friends' houses, so I could cover for a sick employee, or the two o'clock a.m. phone calls from tenants, or the stressed conversations between Phil and me over the latest work issue. (I'm pretty sure they remember eating Hamburger Helper often in those early, lean years!) Henderson Properties has always been an extension of our family. I'm proud of that. Like my family, Henderson

*Like my family, Henderson Properties was built from scratch.*

Properties was built from scratch. No trust funds, no bank loans. We focused our energies on the future ahead of us, and we kept moving in that direction, despite all else.

Shortly before I wrote this book, Phil and I went into Uptown Charlotte for dinner and people watching—not something we do often, but it was such a nice night, we decided it would be fun. We chatted about how things were going personally and professionally. We talked about how far we had come. Our success has pleasantly surprised the two of us. We were content to remain a small business, and we remembered how our goal was to make it so that we might have a staff of twenty. To date, we have more than tripled that number. In the first years of our business we were focused on survival, hiring the right people, managing turnover, and getting our policies and procedures in place. More recently, we've been focused on getting the right people in the right seats and making sure that we inspire and lead these people to greatness within the company. We credit our success to our motivation, accepting challenges as they come our way, admitting when things aren't working, taking time to make decisions, and putting people first. If business leaders begin putting people first and giving back to the community in the way Henderson Properties does, it can change our families, our industries, and our communities.

When a company is built on faith and a people-first attitude, there is a solid foundation that is invaluable to success. I hope this is the Henderson Properties legacy. I hope that people see our sign and go, "That is a great company. They do things so differently over there." We have built much more than a business. We have built a community that I trust our employees are proud of. We don't care about being the biggest. (Though if that happens, it would be awesome!) Bigger does not constitute success. What we care about is our continued growth, our continued success. We want to be the best. I didn't say perfect but know our heart is in the right place. For Phil and me, that success is measured by the number of lives that have been positively affected by our business. I can think of no greater legacy. Our generation was taught to grow up and get a job, probably because of the security in that mind-set. I hope with all my heart our employees think of our company as more than a job and the clients we serve view us as more than a real estate firm. Phil and I have created something from scratch and our greatest rewards will always include our family within the walls of our home and our family within the walls of Henderson Properties.

Our story isn't finished but is taking on a new chapter. I am excited to see where it leads. I think there is still room to grow and evolve so that we're constantly working smarter, not harder. We are in the midst of remodeling the new office, and we are looking at the future with optimism. Why? Because we choose to view it that way. There's more to do, for sure. Phil and I have no plans to retire. Maybe we'll work fewer hours eventually, but I don't ever see full retirement in our futures, which is not a bad thing. We will continue to be at the helm of Henderson Properties, though I am branching out to facilitate more leadership-training courses and speaking engagements. I don't want to be stagnant, so I'm excited to see what the next phase of life will look like for my company, my family, and myself. Our sons have both shown some interest in working at Henderson Properties—but what we really want is that they choose whatever path is right for *them*.

This is a sweet season in my life. I think sometimes the unknowns—or the past—can create fear and doubt, but thanks to my Tuesday group, we are learning a new mind-set: one of positivity and joy. We were meant to live a life of joy and happiness, whether that is in the work place or at home. We can make that happen by maintaining a positive mental attitude, no matter our circumstance. Wake up each morning with feelings of gratitude and anticipation, because today is your day. Live it so that you have no regret and know that what you say and do will positively or negatively, for that matter, affect someone's life. You never know who you may meet, or the opportunities life may present you. Pay attention to every detail and know that as long as you are living and breathing, you have the power to change the way you think and act. What you put in your mind you will ultimately become. We only have the power to change one person. That person is ourselves.

Phil and I never dreamed we would have a business that would have a staff of sixty. We have a good brand, one that we're proud of. I don't take that for granted at all. The brand is still a work in progress. Like on the golf course, you want to keep playing because you love the game. We love the challenge and we enjoy reaping the rewards. It takes work and commitment to build something from scratch that will last.

If your life is full it is easier to have an influence on others. I don't fear the future or the what-ifs anymore. This mindset comes from wisdom and experience. Whatever happens will happen but let's enjoy the ride. Life isn't meant to be driven on a straight road. I look forward to the detours and veering off the beaten path every once in a while. I hope to take others on that path, too. After all, life is meant to be shared—and I thank you for sharing in a small part of our entrepreneurial journey. The rest remains to be seen.

# ABOUT HENDERSON PROPERTIES

-----------------------------------------------------

Henderson Properties is a full-service real estate company founded in 1990, and incorporated in 1998, by Philip and Shelly Henderson in Charlotte, North Carolina. The company provides services to real estate investors, homeowners, tenants, and community associations in the areas of rental property management, leasing, community association management, property maintenance, and home sales.

The founding of Henderson Properties was a result of Phil's personal real estate investment and management activities. When he was asked to manage a colleague's rental properties, a business was born. By 1995, referrals from clients had generated enough rental property management business for Phil to resign from his career in medical equipment sales and make Henderson Properties his full-time job. Within three years, Henderson Properties was managing 100 rental properties; in 2009, the company was managing 330 rental properties across the Charlotte area, and doubled in 2012 to over 770. Henderson Properties is continuing to grow portfolio depth and manages 750+ rental properties, including single family and multi-family properties.

In 1998, Henderson Properties launched its Community Association Management (CAM) division, offering management, accounting, and maintenance services to single-family, townhome, and condominium homeowners associations. In 2006, a Lake Norman office was opened to better serve community associations north of Charlotte. In 2009, the firm acquired On-Call Property Management LLC and in 2013 acquired Faith Management Services. The CAM division now manages 150+ communities.

The Property Maintenance division was founded in 2000 to perform and supervise necessary repairs to the clubhouses and other common areas of the community associations Henderson Properties manages. The maintenance division also offers 24-hour, on-call repair services to its real estate investors and tenants, eliminating the need for rental property owners to become personally involved in performing maintenance repairs. This division is also available to individual homeowners seeking maintenance services for their residences.

In 2007, Henderson Properties added a Real Estate Sales division to assist real estate investors, tenants and homeowners with the purchase and sale of residential property. The division opened a dedicated sales office at 5110 Park Road in Charlotte's Selwyn Terrace shopping center in 2015. In 2017, the number of full-time sales agents has doubled, in large part due to the company's competitive agent benefits package. The sales team markets to current investor and tenant clients as well as the general public. The sales website is www.HendersonHomesCharlotte.com.

Henderson Properties knows the importance of giving back to the Charlotte community. Each year, employees spend hours on an annual food drive benefiting Second Harvest Food Bank of Metrolina and various other local causes. Through employees, tenants, investors, homeowners, HOA Board Members, and the general public, the food drive brings in an average of 2,000 lbs. of food and nonperishable goods for families in the community.

Over the years, Henderson Properties has continued to grow while maintaining its commitment to the firm's original vision: "*To provide real estate services that positively affect the quality of people's lives every day.*" For more information, contact Henderson Properties at 704-535-1122 or www.HendersonProperties.com.

# HENDERSON PROPERTIES AREAS OF EXPERTISE

Henderson Properties is qualified to serve as an expert source on matters related to:

- **Homeowners and Community Association Management**
  - Foreclosures
  - Legal issues, disputes, covenants
  - Financial management / Budgeting
  - Board requirements, roles and duties

- **Rental Property Management and Leasing**
  - Legal requirements including compliance with real estate law and Fair Housing guidelines
  - Tenant issues including qualifying, selecting and servicing tenants
  - Owner issues including financial management and reporting
  - Service and maintenance

- **Residential and Community Maintenance**
  - Maintenance of common areas of community associations in compliance with the community's bylaws and covenants
  - Notification, assessment and dispute resolution for non-compliant homeowners
  - Repairs and improvements for investment property and individual homeowners

- Tips for maintenance and improvements that will increase a property's value
- **Investing/Real Estate Sales**
  - Trends on buying and selling of primary residences
  - Buying, selling and managing residential rental properties
  - How to use an IRA for Investment properties
- **Other Subjects**
  - Issues pertaining to owning, renting, selling, managing, and maintaining residential properties

## FACTS:

**Year Founded:** 1990

**Incorporated:** 1998

**HOAs Managed:** 150+

**Rental Properties Managed:** 750+

**Property Managers:** 17

**Full Time Real Estate Sales Agents:** 12

**Charlotte, N.C. Offices:** 5

**BBB Accredited**

# HENDERSON PROPERTIES DIVISIONS

Henderson Properties has four divisions: Community Association Management, Rental Property Management, Property Maintenance and Renovations, and Real Estate Sales.

## COMMUNITY ASSOCIATION MANAGEMENT

Henderson Properties' Community Association Management division offers a full range of services to homeowners and condominium associations to ensure compliance with governing regulations and provision of exceptional service to property owners. Most community association governing documents allow the community's Board of Directors to hire a management company (Henderson Properties) to perform many of their administrative tasks such as:

- Board and annual meeting management including information preparation, notification, and reporting, as well as training of new board members.

- Compliance with the association's governing documents including regular inspection of the community and resolution of rule violations.

- Community services including responding to inquiries and requests from members and community web site services.

- Financial services, including annual budgeting, collection of assessment and delinquent payments, monthly financial reporting, accounts payable, and facilitation of audits.

- Maintenance and repair of common elements and capital reserve projects, including management of outside contractors, and recommendation of urgent or preventative maintenance.

## RENTAL PROPERTY MANAGEMENT

Henderson Properties' Rental Property Management division provides comprehensive marketing, maintenance, and management services that make renting homes in the Charlotte region profitable and easier for real estate investors and homeowners.

Services include:

- Screening and qualification of tenants, including credit and criminal background checks.

- Preparation and enforcement of lease contracts in compliance with real estate law and Fair Housing guidelines.

- Marketing of rental properties through digital and traditional advertising, including the local Multiple Listing Service (MLS).

- Financial management, including collection and disposition of security deposits and monthly rents, and preparation of monthly and annual income and expense statements.

- Maintenance services, including 24-hour, on-call services, coordination of contractors, and recommendations for preventative maintenance and improvements.

## PROPERTY MAINTENANCE AND RENOVATIONS

Henderson Properties' Property Maintenance division provides and manages repair and maintenance services to community associations, rental property owners, tenants and individual home-owners. Henderson also manages renovation projects for home-owners, investors, and association common areas.

Services include:

- Manage owner and occupant needs for property repair and maintenance, including 24-hour access to maintenance.

- Maintain and repair common elements of community associations in accordance with the standards set by master covenants and by-laws and as directed by the board.

- Recommend, hire, and supervise contractors for major maintenance projects and capital reserve projects.

- Regularly inspect properties and recommend preventative maintenance or other improvements to the community association board or property owner.

- Provide repair and maintenance services to individual homeowners in the Charlotte region.

- Provide renovation and rehabilitation services for investors in preparing properties for rent or to flip.

## REAL ESTATE SALES

Henderson Properties' Real Estate Sales division's office is located in Charlotte's Madison Park neighborhood and fulfills the home buying, selling, and relocation needs for individual homeowners and rental property investors in the Charlotte metro area.

Services include:

- Buying and selling of primary residences and investment properties.

- Buyer assistance on selecting the ideal home based on the buyer's lifestyle, preferences, and needs.

- Seller services including market analysis, price setting, property preparation (including maintenance and repairs), home staging, and marketing.

- Contract negotiation for both buyers and sellers.

For more information about these services, contact Henderson Properties at 704-535-1122 or visit us online at **www.HendersonProperties.com**.

For real estate sales, call 704-544-0253 or visit **HendersonHomesCharlotte.com**.

# COMMUNITY OUTREACH

Henderson Properties is passionate about community outreach and frequently works with the following organizations and professional affiliations in an effort to better Charlotte and its surrounding areas and provide customers with the best real estate experience.

## HENDERSON PROPERTIES COMMUNITY SERVICE PARTNERS

Charlotte Firefighters Association
Christian Library International
Independence Place
Juvenile Diabetes Research Foundation (JDRF)
Kids First of the Carolinas/WBT and John Hancock
Mecklenburg County Shop with a Cop Program
REALTORS® Care Day
Second Harvest Food Bank of Metrolina
Thompson Family Services
Urban Ministry
YMCA

## HENDERSON PROPERTIES PROFESSIONAL AFFILIATIONS

Better Business Bureau (BBB)
Charlotte Chamber of Commerce (C3)
Charlotte Regional Realtor® Association (CRRA)
North Carolina Christian Chamber of Commerce (NC-C3)
Commercial Board of Realtors® (CRCBR)

Community Associations Institute (CAI)
Entrepreneur's Organization (EO)
Greater Charlotte Apartment Association (GCAA)
Home Builders Association of Greater Charlotte (BHAGC)
HOAManagement.com
HOA-USA
National Association of Rental Property Managers (NARPM)
North Carolina Real Estate Commission (NCREC)
Union County Chamber of Commerce (UCC)
York County Chamber of Commerce (YCCoC)